TEN OF ME, ONE OF YOU

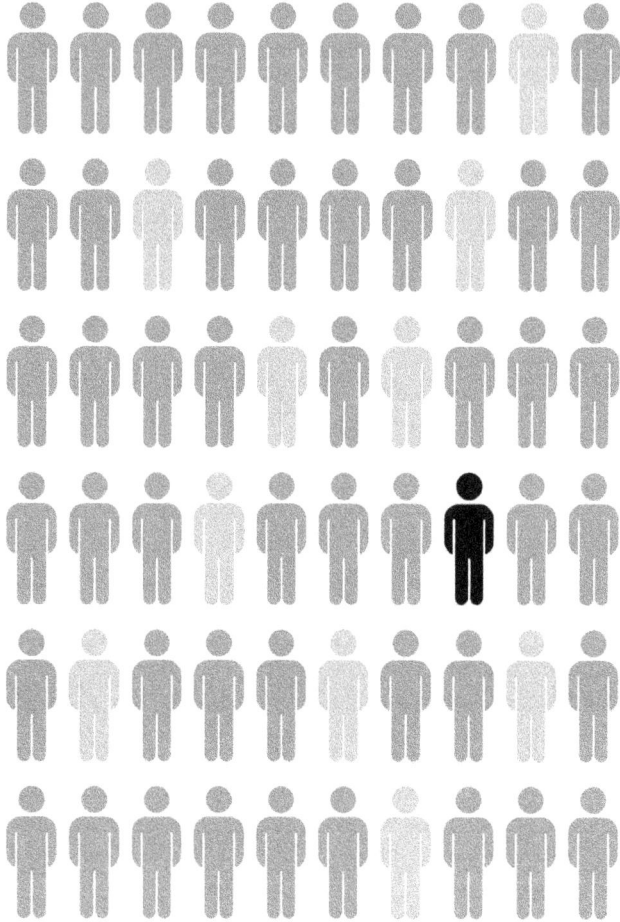

TEN OF ME, ONE OF YOU

How to Lead, Collaborate, and Innovate as a Junior Executive

JESSE L. COOK

TEN OF ME, ONE OF YOU
How to Lead, Collaborate, and Innovate as a Junior Executive

Copyright © 2024 by Jesse L. Cook

Interior Layout and Design by Stephanie Anderson
Book Cover Design by Abigael Elliott

ISBNs:
979-8-89165-147-0 *Paperback*
979-8-89165-148-7 *Hardback*
979-8-89165-146-3 *E-book*

Published by:
Streamline Books
Kansas City, MO
streamlinebookspublishing.com

STREAMLINE
BOOKS

May this book serve as a guiding light for my beloved son, Conner, as he embarks on his career journey. My greatest hope is that the practical tools and insights contained within these pages will help not only him but also current and future junior executives to achieve their full potential.

CONTENTS

The challenge of leadership is to be strong, but not rude; be kind, but not weak; be bold, but not bully; be thoughtful, but not lazy; be humble, but not timid; be proud, but not arrogant; have humor, but without folly.

—JIM ROHN

The Struggles of Leadership

OVER THE YEARS, I've had the privilege of mentoring numerous leaders, guiding them through their career journeys, and helping them to reach executive positions. Whether it's assisting someone in their transition from a senior manager to a director or supporting directors who were once my mentees, the dynamic of mentorship has always fascinated me. It's a two-way street; as much as you're helping someone else grow, they end up enriching your own perspective.

As I've observed various leaders I mentored navigate through organizational changes and promotions, often encountering significant challenges in their new roles, I couldn't help but wonder if I could have supported them better. This led me to contemplate the idea of documenting my journey—the successes, the failures, and the lessons learned.

I wanted to not only analyze my own experiences but also gather insights from other leaders I've collaborated with, including a few of my former bosses, to see what worked well and what didn't work. As someone who has served as an operational director for more than a decade, I attribute my success to constantly evolving and adapting to new challenges, and we can't adapt unless we understand and embrace all of the lessons learned along the way.

Furthermore, I believe it's important to share these experiences because executive leadership offers little room for complacency. If you're not performing, there's a swift exit waiting. So, my goal in writing this book was simple: if my documented experiences and lessons learned could help even just one person navigate through their own leadership challenges, then it would be worth the effort. After all, in the realm of leadership, you rarely face a problem that hasn't been encountered by other leaders before you. By sharing our experiences, we can learn from each other's solutions and strategies.

Additionally, my son, who is currently eleven years old, served as a significant inspiration for this book. As I've witnessed his enthusiasm for learning, I have come to realize the importance of passing down my knowledge and experiences to him. By bringing him into executive meetings and letting him witness firsthand the intricacies of team dynamics, I want to make sure that my wisdom is preserved for him, even when he's forty. If this book can serve as a guide for him or anyone else, then I will consider it a success beyond any other measure.

Beyond my son, this book was written especially for junior executives, though some of the advice applies to leadership more broadly. Each leadership role comes with its own set of trials; it's like a custom-made roller-coaster ride. However, I know from experience (my own and others) that junior executives grapple with some uniquely difficult challenges.

In fact, the title of this book, *Ten of Me, One of You*, was inspired by the fact that junior executives are quite rare and deal with some unique demands. In my specific field, there are only ten people who do what I do (thus, "ten of me"). It's a rare leadership position, so the difficulties are not often addressed in leadership books. I want to tackle them head-on.

For starters, junior executives often find themselves in a tight spot, caught between the demands of the business, the expectations of C-level executives, and the needs of frontline employees. Pleasing everyone is like trying to juggle water balloons and cacti at the same time—they're polar opposites. How can you possibly bridge that gap?

In my line of work, which is technical operations, the challenge is even more pronounced because we have to make certain that we have enough skilled leaders who understand the nitty-gritty of our technical setup. And those leaders also need to ensure they've got a solid support network in place because, let's face it, things break down, and when they break, there's always a human touch needed to fix them. But fixing broken things isn't enough. Those same leaders also have to figure out how to prevent similar breakdowns from happening again.

My Own Roller-Coaster Ride

Like most leaders, I came up through the ranks myself once upon a time, so I have experienced my own personal journey through the thorny thicket of leadership challenges. One of the biggest struggles I had early on was trying to figure out how to simplify complex issues. As a technical operations director, I often found myself knee-deep in conversations with top-tier engineers and developers, discussing intricate technical details, but when

I had to bring these issues to the C-suite, it felt like speaking a different language.

C-suite executives are not often tech whizzes, and that's fine. It was on me to break down these complex topics into bite-size pieces they could understand.

Another major hurdle I faced was dealing with staff reductions. Nobody likes layoffs, but it's part of business sometimes. The trick is to maintain a strong bench, ensuring you still have the talent and resources to support your customers effectively. It's like balancing on a tightrope—one wrong move and you're in freefall.

Those are just a couple of examples of the battles I've fought on my journey through leadership. It's been a wild ride, to say the least, but every challenge has been a learning opportunity. And if my experiences can help someone else navigate their own leadership maze, then it's all been worth it.

What's in Store?

So, what's in store for you in the upcoming chapters? Let's break it down into nine impactful sections. First off, we're diving into the realm of **culture**. How do you keep the vibes positive in your organization, even when you're hit with tough stuff like layoffs? We'll dissect that, along with the importance of **collaboration and communication**. Bringing teams together and ensuring leaders are on the same page is crucial to effective leadership.

Next up, we'll tackle the art of **delegation**. As a new leader, I learned the hard way that you can't do it all (no matter how much you might want to). We'll discuss how to manage and prioritize tasks, delegate effectively, and avoid burning out your team.

Then, we'll get into **surpassing goals**. Setting targets is one thing, but exceeding them is a whole other ball game. How do you set your yearly goals, quarterly goals, or even monthly goals and then inspire your people to get beyond them? We'll explore strategies like automation and fostering a culture of innovation to push past those benchmarks.

Moving on, we'll talk about **building and maintaining your talent pool**. Whether it's hiring fresh faces, rearranging your resources, or providing opportunities for continuous learning, nurturing talent is key to any leader's success. This is about maintaining a pipeline of resources: how to build talent, when to hire, when to reorganize, and so on.

We'll also dive into **maintaining a balance between stability and innovation**. In my role, maintaining a stable network is crucial, but so is staying ahead of the curve with new ideas and approaches. I can't allow my customers to suffer. I want them to have the best and most reliable service, so I have to ensure consistency and stability. But I also need innovative talent with fresh ideas because we have to be forward-looking. This is a tricky balancing act.

Then, let's talk about **crisis management**. When things hit the fan, how do you keep your cool and guide your team through the storm? We'll explore staying neutral, leveraging expertise, and troubleshooting like a pro. When stuff breaks, people get stressed out, and they often become emotional. Somehow, you have to become the calm, confident leader who can keep things on track. At the same time, you need to leverage the expertise your teams have to find problems, fix them, and then determine the root cause. Another tricky balancing act.

Troubleshooting is another topic we'll delve into. From narrowing down issues to leveraging technical expertise, I will equip you with the tools to tackle any problem head-on. You have to put your highly technical hat on and understand what your teams are telling you to drive troubleshooting in the right direction.

And finally, we'll wrap it all up with a focus on **building for tomorrow and not today.** In an ever-changing landscape, staying ahead of the curve is essential. We'll discuss preparing for technological shifts and ensuring seamless transitions to keep your customers happy.

In the world of networks—my world—one thing is consistent, and that's change. People change, and technology changes. We have seen a tremendous amount of technological advancement in the twenty-four years I've worked in this industry. Consider the way home internet has changed. Internet speed has increased exponentially in the last two decades. In the early years of my career, entire data centers had the internet speed that almost every home has in America today.

But the pace of change is not limited to the world of networks. In fact, things have changed dramatically in almost every industry, and you're responsible as a leader to support the business even as the environment changes all around you. How in the world do you keep your eyes forward while maintaining what you have? How do you stay ready to take on the next new thing?

It's just like your home computer. It lasts a couple of years, and then it's time to swap it for a newer and more powerful model. How do you know when you're ready to make the swap? How do you know which new systems are right for you? Are you ready for the changes? Does the upgrade have a learning curve? These are the kinds of questions leaders have to be able to answer because, if you can't, it might negatively impact the customer. And the customer comes before everything.

We're going to cover all of these topics because, as I've learned over the years, these are the things that are most crucial for leadership, especially junior executives. Along the way, I will also share some quotes from a variety of gifted and smart leaders I've interviewed on these topics. I found what they had to say both challenging and compelling, and I think you will too. So get ready to level up your leadership game, and let's get started!

Being a great place to work is the difference between being a good company and a great company.

—**BRIAN KRISTOFEK,**
PRESIDENT AND CEO,
UPSHOT

CHAPTER 1

Nurturing Culture

ACCORDING TO GALLUP, employees who feel strongly connected to their company culture are 37 percent more likely to thrive on the job and 68 percent less likely to feel frequently burned out at work. Additionally, employees who believe the culture is positive are 3.8 times more likely to be engaged.[1]

So, with that in mind, what role do leaders play in creating that kind of culture for their teams? Starting from the frontline leadership and moving up to the junior executive level, the game changes as you climb that ladder. Let's break it down.

As a frontline leader, your main gig is your people, so they should make up about 75 percent of your focus, while the business side takes up the remaining 25 percent. It's all about showing your team they matter and you've got their backs, because when you prioritize business needs over your people, it's like putting the cart before the horse—things just don't roll right.

Now, when you step up to managing managers, that ratio shifts a bit. You're still mostly focused on your frontline crew, but now the split is more like 65 percent for them, 35 percent for the business. You're still down in the trenches with your team, tackling challenges and making sure they've got what they need to shine. And you are constantly answering questions like these:

- How am I investing in my people?
- How am I giving them what they need?
- Am I scheduling regular one-on-one meetings?
- Am I listening to them?
- Am I listening to their challenges?
- Am I working through problems?
- Am I helping when people need to go on bereavement or get seriously ill?
- How does this impact our resource pool?
- Am I shifting my team around so I can handle expected outcomes?
- How do I handle the unexpected ones?

Your focus is still primarily on the individual, not so much the business. But when you hit the junior executive level—think director or vice president—it becomes a 50-50 split. In other words, half your time is about hitting those business objectives, and the other half is about nurturing your people.

This requires a delicate dance. You have to make sure the company's goals are met while also fostering a positive team culture. Somehow, you have to do both equally well while also managing the expectations of different leaders. When you manage to strike that balance just right, you create a vibe where everyone feels valued and supported. Your employees don't feel isolated and alone. They see that you are investing in them, and they feel motivated to keep delivering their best.

That's the secret sauce to a killer team culture: leaders who invest in their people. So it's extremely important to get that mix just right.

An Innovative and Positive Culture

When you cultivate a positive culture, magic happens. People start collaborating like never before. Sure, they'll come together for the good stuff, but even the not-so-great stuff gets a spotlight. That's where the real magic of a positive culture shines.

See, when team members feel safe to speak their minds, even about the not-so-great parts of your processes, that's when you really begin to see the impact of your culture. Maybe you've introduced some red tape, and you had valid business reasons for doing so. However, because you have a positive culture, your people feel empowered to say, "Hey, this red tape is killing our productivity, and here's why."

It's like a wake-up call straight to the gut. Sometimes, I'm surprised by what I hear from my team members, but it's important that they feel safe to share it. It might just save the business!

On one occasion, I discovered that people were having to work on Saturdays because of a rule I'd put in place. That had not been my intention, so I quickly rectified the situation. However, if I hadn't already nurtured a positive culture, people might not have felt free to share their concerns with me. Thus, the problem might never have been resolved, devastating team morale and negatively affecting performance over time.

So, what does an innovative and positive culture look like? Well, for starters, you've got a team with sky-high morale. They're not just coworkers; they're collaborators who are working together at every level of the hierarchy. From frontline leaders down to the tech whizzes, everyone has a voice at the table.

As leaders, it's easy to fall into the trap of thinking you've got all the answers, but if I've learned anything at all over the years, I've learned that you're never the smartest person in the room. When you bring everyone together in a healthy culture where they feel safe to share, you get a brainstorming bonanza. Sure, you may hear ten different answers to the same problem, but somewhere in there lies the gem of an idea that's going to make all the difference.

With a positive culture where people feel valued and heard, those game-changing ideas start flowing like a river. Whether it's tackling the small stuff or wrestling with the big challenges, a positive culture sets the stage for innovation and success.

Unfortunately, it is harder than ever to foster an innovative and positive culture because so many companies are managing 24-7 geo-redundant teams. *Geo-redundant* means two or more data centers that can serve the same traffic. I've got team members scattered across the East Coast, West Coast, and smack dab in the central part of the country. I've even had times where I had team members spanning across continents, from Asia to Europe and back to the United States.

Why is this such a challenge? For one simple reason: lack of face-to-face interaction. This whole debate about remote work versus in-person work? Yeah, I've heard it all. And trust me: I've got a foot in both camps. I have people working remotely from home, I have people in the office, and then there are team members who are spread across the globe, never meeting face-to-face. And let me tell you, that water cooler talk? Those impromptu brainstorming sessions? They're a luxury my team doesn't get to enjoy.

Imagine this scenario: I'm sitting in an office in New York City, leading a team that's scattered across the globe. When we have a team meeting, half the crew is just a bunch of faces on a screen, whether they've dialed in from home or from the office. It's like they're worlds away, missing out on that one-on-one connection I have with the folks sitting right there in front of me.

That's where the real challenge lies. As leaders, we have to invest time in our teams, no matter where they are. We have to foster that positive culture and listen for those game-changing ideas, even if it means doing it all over a video call.

But it's all too easy to default to the folks who are in the room and forget about those who aren't physically present. That's why intentional pauses, calling on remote team members, and encouraging them to speak up are all vital parts of the game. Everyone needs to feel valued and heard, whether they're in the room or halfway across the globe pulling a night shift.

Appreciating Everyone

Managing a 24-7 geo-redundant team is challenging, but it's worth the intentional effort to bring everyone together and still somehow instill a shared sense of culture. You have people working around the clock, across different time zones, and somehow, you have to accommodate all of them. That means, above all, making sure every voice is heard, every idea is considered, whether it's positive feedback or constructive criticism. Because as a wise leader once told me, "Feedback is a gift."

I've had team members who let loose with frustration during meetings because they felt like their contributions weren't valued. But you know what? That feedback, as tough as it was to hear, was invaluable. It pushed me to do better, to make certain that every member of my team felt valued and appreciated, no matter where they are in the world.

If you're going to maintain a positive culture even though your people are spread out all over the place, it's essential to establish a solid structure for communication and collaboration across all levels of leadership. No one should feel left out, regardless of where they're located. That means dedicating time for one-on-one interactions with each team member. This is a nonnegotiable— everyone deserves that individual attention.

Then you need to make sure everyone feels connected, even if they're miles apart. You can achieve this through regular team meetings, spontaneous catch-ups, emails, or even instant messaging. Sometimes, especially when dealing with a widely dispersed team, it's more practical to rely on virtual tools like WebEx, even if some people are sitting side by side. The key is to foster a sense of unity and make sure that every voice is heard, whether it's coming from across the office or across the globe.

Remember: your goal is to create an environment where every team member feels valued and included. After all, it's their ideas and expertise that drive innovation and success. If you inadvertently shut people out, you're missing out on a wealth of potential solutions and insights. That's why it's so important to actively seek input from everyone, regardless of their physical location.

Being geo-redundant certainly presents its challenges, but with a well-thought-out plan and a commitment to inclusivity, you can overcome them and maintain a positive and innovative culture across the board.

The foundation of a strong culture is communication at all levels. Frank, consistent, and transparent messages, through a variety of channels, are the most important aspects. I like to use email and roundtable discussions periodically, and I frequently walk around the office to have impromptu conversations as opposed to formal meetings with presentations. By modeling this behavior at the executive level, directors and managers have a guide to further the messages through the channels they are most comfortable with for additional frequency and repetition.

—**JOE MEYER,** VP of Network Operations

Maintaining Positivity

It's one thing to lay the groundwork for a positive culture. It's another thing altogether to maintain it and keep it going, especially with a widely dispersed team. It's a challenge, but one that I believe can be tackled with a clear plan and unwavering commitment.

First things first, you need to come up with a solid plan for communication and collaboration and then stick to it. Share that plan with your superiors and seek their input. After all, they might have valuable insights or strategies that you haven't considered. We will talk a lot more about communication and collaboration in the next chapter.

Accountability is key. As a leader, it's your responsibility to ensure that every team member feels included and valued, regardless of their location. That means holding each other accountable for decisions that impact your geographically dispersed teams. If a meeting is scheduled at a time that doesn't work for everyone, it's up to you to speak up and suggest alternatives. Whether that means adjusting the timing or scheduling multiple sessions to accommodate different time zones, it's essential to prioritize inclusivity.

Even as a director, I have to be constantly mindful of the needs of our geographically dispersed resources and make certain that our leadership team reflects that awareness. It's about fostering a culture where everyone feels empowered to voice their concerns and hold each other to account for creating an environment where every team member feels valued and included.

This might take a lot of hard work, but in my experience, it's well worth it. The advantages of cultivating a positive and innovative culture are game-changing.

First and foremost, when everyone feels like they have a voice and their ideas are valued, you begin uncovering hidden treasures. Among a thousand ideas, there's bound to be a few real gems— an innovative solution or approach that could revolutionize how you do business. These are the ideas that often come from unexpected places and perspectives, ideas that you might never have considered on your own. And the best part? Many of these ideas are surprisingly low cost to implement but can yield significant benefits for the entire organization.

Here's the catch: none of these brilliant ideas will surface without a positive culture where people feel empowered to speak up and contribute. It's what I like to call "servant leadership," where leaders prioritize serving and empowering their teams. While it's true that a leader can't dedicate 100 percent of their time to their team because of the demands of running a business, you can (and must) carve out dedicated time for them each day. It's in these moments that those game-changing ideas often emerge.

However, fostering a positive culture isn't just about generating innovative ideas; it's also about retaining top talent. Happy employees who feel valued and connected to their colleagues are more likely to stick around for the long haul. Through collaboration and relationship building, even across different locations, teams can form strong bonds that enhance productivity and problem-solving.

On the flip side, a negative culture breeds isolation and stagnation. When employees feel disconnected from their leaders and colleagues, they're less inclined to share ideas or go above and beyond their basic responsibilities. This siloed mentality stifles innovation and ultimately poses a risk to the organization's success.

So, by prioritizing a positive and innovative culture, you not only unlock the potential for groundbreaking ideas but also cultivate a work environment where employees thrive and your organization can flourish.

No [person] will make a great business who wants to do it all [themselves] or to get all the credit for doing it.

—STEVE JOBS

CHAPTER 2

Communication and Collaboration

O NE OF THE biggest challenges leaders face is getting diverse teams or different departments within an organization to work together and communicate well. There's a natural human tendency to create little silos where we can work in isolation with our own "people," however we define that word. This tendency has only gotten worse in recent years with the rise of remote work. But when departments are siloed, work becomes hindered, processes become inefficient, and a lot of great ideas are never shared or realized.

It's up to leaders like us to break down these silos, and junior executives in particular often play a vital role in cultivating collaboration and fostering communication within and across departments.

To do that, I encourage leaders to regularly and earnestly promote cross-functional collaboration between teams while, at the same time, facilitating opportunities for employees from disparate departments to engage in projects, initiatives, and objectives together. These kinds of collaborative efforts do more to dismantle silos than just about anything else, especially when your teams begin to discover how much more effectively they can tackle challenges and reach objectives by sharing their various skill sets.

Put simply: make it a priority to create a collaborative environment that spans departmental boundaries, and then start actively uniting diverse groups toward shared goals.

Additionally, as a leader, you need to begin fostering open communication within and between departments. Effective communication is a linchpin for successful collaboration. I always encourage leaders to advocate for transparent communication by emphasizing its pivotal role in establishing trust within teams.

Of course, it's not enough to simply promote open communication. You also need to provide teams with the necessary tools and resources to support individuals in honing their communication skills. On diverse teams, individuals may have very different communication styles and preferences, which can make it hard for them to relate to one another. However, by championing open dialogue and providing resources and opportunities, leaders can empower their teams to navigate these challenges and cultivate stronger working relationships.

Lead by example! Regardless of where you are in the hierarchy, leaders set the tone by demonstrating exemplary communication practices. For example, you can send regular organization-wide emails that demonstrate transparency and keep everyone informed. Frontline leaders, in particular, have plenty of opportunities to model collaborative behavior during team meetings, striking a delicate balance between encouraging participation and preventing dominance in discussions.

When you, as a leader, foster a culture of trust, transparency, and inclusivity within your organization and across your teams, you proactively promote collaboration and communication. Through your actions, you get to inspire and guide your teams toward achieving collective objectives and drive success across departments. What a privilege and what an opportunity! Make the most of it.

Getting People to Talk

Fostering collaboration and communication across departments and teams is a challenge I dealt with often during my time as a junior executive, but I've successfully overcome the challenge. I've already shared some tips and tactics, but now I want to share a specific example of how I did it.

In my current role, I am specifically accountable for operations, overseeing the maintenance of the network. For example, earlier this morning (as I write this chapter), I was engaged in a call with my lab teams. My responsibility includes ensuring the functionality of all lab equipment and network connectivity, and unfortunately, the lab teams were encountering issues due to capacity limitations, which caused their network equipment to struggle to meet their demands.

In response, I initiated dialogue with three of my engineering counterparts. We discussed the challenges faced from a production standpoint and explored potential solutions, ranging from addressing capacity constraints by redesigning network configurations to reallocating traffic or considering hardware upgrades. Rather than dictating a specific approach, I focused on fostering collaboration and inviting input from all stakeholders, from team leaders to frontline engineers.

By encouraging an open exchange of ideas and involving all relevant parties in the decision-making process, I contributed to our culture of collective problem-solving. This approach not only facilitated effective communication but also broke down barriers between departments, and it promoted a sense of ownership and cooperation in devising solutions.

Ultimately, this experience serves as a testament to the power of collaborative efforts in overcoming challenges and driving organizational success.

> Breaking down organizational silos and supporting cross-functional collaboration can be a huge accelerator.
>
> —BRIAN KING,
> CIO and COO of Technology

Why Collaboration Is So Difficult

So, why exactly is it so difficult for many business leaders, especially at the junior executive level, to get departments or teams to collaborate and communicate effectively? I think the primary issue is the lack of effort from leaders to create and maintain open communication channels.

When communication channels aren't kept open across different departments, silos tend to form naturally over time, and a lack of communication contributes to a lack of collaboration. If people aren't talking, then they're probably not working together either. Therefore, I believe open communication should be championed from the top down. If executives, including junior executives, fail to foster this communication, it's likely that their subordinates will follow suit.

Consequently, engineers, technicians, and frontline leaders will find it challenging to collaborate with other groups, especially while dealing with their own busy schedules and individual objectives. When communication isn't prioritized at the top level, the avenues for collaboration at every organizational tier diminish.

And if there's no collaboration with other departments, then it's almost impossible to establish a shared vision. Creating such a vision makes sure that everyone is working toward a common goal. While it's understandable that frontline leaders, senior leaders, directors, vice presidents, and even the C-suite may each have their own visions, alignment is essential to ensure that these visions converge toward the same destination.

This is particularly important when different business units have distinct responsibilities. For instance, as I said, my role involves network maintenance while others focus on network construction. Without alignment, we risk pursuing divergent paths. However, by aligning our visions and leveraging collaboration, we can collectively work toward shared objectives, thereby fostering communication across departments.

Tools for Breaking Down Silos

Any department within a company can become siloed, and it can indeed be challenging to break down these silos. One effective approach is to leverage the tools available across the network. In the realm of technology, tools play a crucial role in breaking down existing silos but also preventing silos from being built in the first place.

Whether it's Google, Skype, WebEx, or numerous others, each department tends to have its own preferences and favored tools. To foster collaboration, it's essential to understand the tools used by other departments and align communication channels accordingly.

This alignment is particularly critical at the leadership level, especially among directors. For instance, if one department utilizes Microsoft Teams while another prefers Slack, ensuring seamless communication can be a real challenge if they're not on the same platform. Although email remains a default option, technological advancements increasingly necessitate quick, real-time conversations. If you align tools across different business units, you will make certain that collaboration flows smoothly not only among leaders but also across teams and individual contributors.

COMMUNICATION AND COLLABORATION   17

We went through a similar journey when we were using Microsoft Teams. The company purchased WebEx, so some groups began using WebEx Meetings while other groups continued to use Teams. However, in order to foster and encourage communication, we decided to move all of our groups onto the same platform—in this case, WebEx. The full transition took a little time, but it was worth the effort in the end.

Even if your teams or departments are using the same platform, you may begin collaborating with third-party vendors or contractors who use different communication platforms. I've dealt with situations where we were paying third-party business consultants millions of dollars to develop something for us or deal with some technical function for a period of months, but they were using a different communication platform than us.

For example, maybe they were using Skype, and suddenly, in order to collaborate with them, we had to install Skype. Otherwise, they would be sitting in a siloed group outside of regular communication with our own teams.

We use a lot of different vendors, such as Cisco, Nokia, and Ericsson, and each of them has their own communication and collaboration tools. If possible, we try to align them to our tools from the beginning so collaboration is seamless.

Ultimately, you need to make sure that you have effective collaboration happening across not only internal business groups but also external business groups that provide value to the overall business.

> Encourage collaboration at all levels by modeling the behavior at the executive level and by bringing groups of managers and individual contributors together to facilitate problem-solving. Pose the problem statement and goals to those closest to the work and allow them the freedom to come up with solutions that will actually work in practice.
> —**JOE MEYER,** VP of Network Operations

The Connection between Collaboration and Communication

Clear communication channels are fundamental in paving the way for effective collaboration. Without clear communication protocols in place, cohesion begins to unravel. In order to align all of your teams toward common goals, I recommend regular meetings, consistent messaging apps, and shared problem-management tools. Divergent tools can hinder collaboration and communication, so strive to establish standardized channels and tools across all of your teams.

At the same time, make it a priority to foster a culture of open communication where employees begin to feel valued, trusted, and empowered to share ideas, concerns, and feedback. It is particularly important to create a safe and inclusive environment where feedback is welcomed and regarded as a gift, not merely tolerated, even when some of that feedback may be difficult to hear. Building trust and promoting collaboration are intrinsically linked to cultivating an environment where open communication flourishes.

Find ways to leverage technology in order to foster collaboration. With the plethora of technological tools available, it's worthwhile to invest in good tools that will facilitate seamless communication and collaboration. I recommend prioritizing email, chat messaging, and video conferencing. Then align your technology across different business units, third-party collaborators, and internal teams. This will enhance communication and encourage collaboration, driving collective success across the entire organization.

No person will make a great business who wants to do it all themself or get all the credit.

—ANDREW CARNEGIE

CHAPTER 3

The Art of Delegation

MANY LEADERS, ESPECIALLY newer ones or those recently promoted to director or vice president roles, struggle to prioritize tasks and delegate them effectively, even though this is an essential skill for leaders to develop. It is absolutely vital for any leader to learn to identify and differentiate the essential tasks that require their attention and those that can be delegated to other team members.

After all, as leaders, we all have limited time, and we can only give our full attention to a certain number of tasks. It is most effective, therefore, to focus on tasks that are aligned with your qualifications while delegating others to individuals whose skill sets are better suited for them.

For each task you delegate, you need to develop a delegation plan. A delegation plan should identify the right person for the task, set clear expectations and deadlines, and provide adequate resources to ensure successful completion.

Additionally, you need to monitor progress. That does not mean micromanaging the task! Rather, it involves tracking milestones and receiving updates to make certain tasks stay on track. That way, if deviations occur, adjustments can be made promptly, such as providing additional resources or support.

Failing to Prioritize

But it's not easy to delegate when you don't know which tasks to prioritize. In my experience, leaders who lack clarity about which tasks to prioritize tend to share vague ideas without a clear plan for execution. This leads to confusion among the team about what to focus on, which can result in delays and mistakes, ultimately impacting productivity.

A lack of clarity often leads to ineffective delegation. Many leaders, especially newer ones, may delegate too much, or too little, or they may fail to delegate to the right people based on their skill sets. They may delegate critical tasks that are better left to leaders, or they may delegate without providing well-defined expectations. In all of these instances, they can leave team members feeling overwhelmed, underutilized, or lacking support.

To prioritize the right tasks and delegate effectively to the right people, you need to align priorities with goals and skill sets with the needs of the task. Leaders sometimes prioritize tasks that are urgent but not necessarily important in the long run. Instead, make sure to focus on tasks that contribute to long-term objectives rather than getting caught up in immediate concerns. Additionally, make sure to hand tasks to the people who are best suited for them so they are positioned for success. Then set clear milestones so progress can be tracked and make sure all tasks receive the necessary resources and support if you want to guarantee success in the long term.

Put simply, you must prioritize tasks with clarity, delegate effectively based on skill sets, align priorities with long-term goals, provide resources and support, and track milestones to drive success.

> Openly placing trust in someone and providing ongoing support can be a huge motivator for individuals and teams.
>
> **—BRIAN KING,**
> CIO and COO of Technology

Why Do We Resist?

Many leaders feel a strange, instinctive resistance to delegating tasks, especially important ones. A study conducted by the University of California, Berkeley, revealed that 60 percent of managers believe they don't delegate enough.[2] In my experience, this isn't limited to people at the management level. Senior leaders struggle to delegate just as much, if not more. Even when they know they need to do it, they have a hard time embracing it. Why is this? What are they afraid of?

I believe leaders often resist delegating because they fear losing control over the outcome of the task, or they worry that it won't be completed to their standards. This fear may stem from a lack of trust in their teams. They just don't think their team members will do a good enough job.

Sometimes, a leader may fear that they will make team or team members shoulder too much responsibility. They worry that if they delegate tasks to already busy people, it will increase the chances of failure and potentially make them look like ineffective leaders. This fear of looking ineffective is prevalent among leaders at all levels, both new and seasoned, which just highlights the need for proven delegation strategies even more.

Additionally, some technical leaders struggle to relinquish control, particularly concerning the technical aspects of their roles that they excel at or enjoy. Why give up doing something that you like doing? Engineers transitioning into leadership roles may find it hard to let go of hands-on technical tasks, such as logging into equipment or analyzing data, because they feel competent in these areas and hesitate to delegate them to others. This reluctance to delegate technical work can persist even as these leaders advance in their careers, but it will ultimately hinder their ability to focus on broader leadership responsibilities.

Overcoming this common resistance to delegation requires that you, as a leader, first recognize the importance of letting go and then take intentional action to begin entrusting tasks to capable team members. No matter how difficult it may be to let go of direct responsibility for a task, it is essential for effective leadership and organizational success.

Struggling to Transition

I once worked alongside a highly technical coworker who was responsible for managing routers, switches, and firewalls. This individual was eventually promoted to a managerial position overseeing a team of fifteen engineers, each with many years of experience. Despite having five-plus years of leadership experience upon joining the organization, this new leader struggled to transition from a technical role to a leadership role.

Even as a manager, when we encountered network issues or other kinds of technical problems, he would still resort to logging into the equipment himself and challenging engineers on technical matters rather than providing the necessary resources and support for the team to address the issues collaboratively themselves. While it's crucial for leaders to understand the technical aspects of their team's work, it's equally important to trust and empower your team members to utilize their specialized skill sets effectively. Entrust them with the task, then let go of it.

Unfortunately, this individual found it extremely difficult to strike a balance between his own technical expertise and his role as a leader. This struggle ultimately led to increasing difficulties in his managerial position. He simply couldn't bring himself to stop meddling, and it caused resentment with his team. Eventually, as a direct result, he left the company to pursue an engineering role elsewhere.

It was disappointing to witness this outcome because he had such potential, in my opinion. However, it serves as a reminder of the importance of effectively transitioning from a technical role to a leadership role in a managerial position.

His struggle was not unique. On another occasion, I worked with two directors, one of whom had ascended from a highly technical role to the pinnacle of technical expertise as a systems architect. Moving into leadership, he assumed the role of a director, and while he gladly seized the opportunity afforded to him, he began to struggle with delegating tasks appropriately.

Because of his profound technical background, he tended to delve excessively into the minutiae of tasks that should have been delegated to other skilled people. Even when a task was assigned to someone else and successfully completed, he often requested a ton of additional details and then provided an unnecessary amount of feedback, which inevitably led to a long cycle of revisions and rework. Over time, this approach fostered growing mistrust among both his team members and fellow leaders, devastating morale.

The lack of clear expectations and generous delegation caused a detrimental ping-pong effect within the organization. His struggle to let go of his technical inclinations exacerbated the issue, resulting in confusion and inefficiency. And since the organization lacked a culture of trust and open discussion, the situation was allowed to continue to fester far too long.

In order to address this, senior leaders would have had to empower technical resources to provide technical answers while setting clear expectations from the outset. That's an approach that would have contributed to collaboration while minimizing unnecessary rework.

I once had an experience with an engineering director where we flew out to Cisco to explore new networking solutions. During the visit, Cisco demonstrated some of their latest tool capabilities tailored specifically for engineers. As we examined the tool, I vividly recall sitting next to this director who remarked, "I'll only trust this tool when I log into it and actually work on the equipment."

That attitude right there is a problem. As leaders, we have to learn to embrace the fact that there's no need for us to intervene in all of the technical aspects handled by engineers. Delegating such tasks demonstrates trust and empowers the team to deliver quality results. As David Ogilvy put it, "Hire people who are better than you are, then leave them to get on with it." In other words, trust your people to do the work!

The Dangers of Ineffective Delegation

As a leader, the dangers of poor task prioritization and ineffective delegation cannot be overstated. These issues directly impact the functionality of your organization as a whole. When tasks are not properly prioritized, critical issues may not receive the attention they require, potentially leading to system downtime and reduced efficiency. In turn, this can negatively impact the organization's bottom line, as operational disruptions affect customer satisfaction and retention.

Furthermore, ineffective delegation often results in team members feeling overwhelmed, leading to burnout and diminished performance. High turnover may ensue, resulting in the loss of valuable talent and skill sets that have been cultivated over time. This creates a detrimental cycle that can have long-lasting effects on the organization.

To mitigate these risks, it is imperative for directors to prioritize tasks based on their importance and urgency, and to delegate them to team members with the appropriate skill sets and expertise. By balancing the workload and empowering the right individuals, you make sure that tasks are completed successfully and that the organization operates smoothly. Thus, effective task prioritization and delegation are essential components of successful leadership in any organization.

> Err on the side of delegating. The experts are closest to the work, and more often than not, they simply need the freedom to arrive at solutions directly. Save executive involvement for escalated situations and tough decision-making, making sure to take into account the feedback from the front line.
>
> **—JOE MEYER,**
> VP of Network Operations

Tips for Prioritizing Tasks

Here are some tips for prioritizing tasks:

First, start by identifying the most urgent tasks. This could include those tasks with impending deadlines, issues requiring immediate attention, or tasks critical to the business's functioning. Prioritize these tasks accordingly.

Second, consider the importance of each task. While some tasks may not be urgent, they could be vital for the overall success of the business. Evaluate the impact of each task and prioritize accordingly.

Third, break down larger tasks into smaller ones. Breaking down large tasks into smaller, more manageable ones helps prevent them from becoming overwhelming and allows for more efficient completion.

Fourth, consider your team's strengths and weaknesses. Recognize that team members bring different strengths to the table and assign tasks accordingly. Leverage their strengths to ensure tasks are completed effectively, and consider tasks that may help improve weaknesses as opportunities for growth and development within the team.

Finally, be flexible and adaptable. Priorities can shift rapidly in dynamic environments. Stay flexible and ready to adjust to changing priorities, ensuring that urgent needs are addressed promptly, even if it means shifting focus from previously prioritized tasks.

When priorities change, you have to adjust your task list accordingly. Sometimes, this means giving more time to certain tasks. It may mean acknowledging that you won't meet a milestone due to shifting business needs, and that's OK. Being reasonable is key. Instead of insisting on deadlines that are no longer feasible, acknowledge the changes and adjust expectations accordingly.

Flexibility and adaptability are essential. There may be times when meeting deadlines becomes impossible, and everyone understands that. However, as a leader, it's your responsibility to find solutions and make certain that tasks are completed effectively, even in challenging circumstances. Most of the time, you can find a way to navigate through these changes and keep the process moving forward smoothly.

- Identify the most urgent tasks.
- Consider the importance of each task, even if they aren't urgent.
- Break down larger tasks into smaller ones.
- Consider your team's strengths and weaknesses.
- Be flexible and adaptable.

Tips for Delegating Tasks

Now, here are some tips for effective delegation:

First, before delegating a task to somebody, make sure you have a clear understanding of what needs to be done and what the desired outcome is, and then communicate that clearly to the person that you're delegating it to. This guarantees that everyone's on the same page and there's no confusion about what is expected.

Second, make sure to choose the right person for the task. Delegating to the right person is key to ensuring the task is completed successfully. Do they have the right skill set, experience, and bandwidth to complete the task with excellence? Consider their current workload. Just piling somebody up with work doesn't give you consistent success over time.

Finally, and perhaps most importantly, provide the ongoing support and feedback they need to succeed. Set milestones, make sure those milestones are hit, and offer help if they aren't.

Even though you're taking the task off your own plate, you need to be there for the person you delegate it to. Help them stay on track, make them feel supported, and make any necessary adjustments along the way. As we already mentioned, be flexible.

This is a good opportunity for you, as a leader, to provide recognition and constructive feedback. Tell people when they're doing a great job. And if they're struggling, say, "This isn't going so well. Let's figure out together what we can do to get you back on track."

Feedback is a gift. Yes, sometimes you have to tell people things they don't want to hear, but if you've fostered a culture of trust and provided adequate support and encouragement, then it can lead to greater outcomes, as well as personal development for the individual.

- Make sure you have a clear understanding of what needs to be done.
- Choose the right person for the task.
- Provide ongoing support and feedback.

Trust gives you the permission to give people direction, get everyone aligned, and give them the energy to go get the job done.

—DOUGLAS CONANT

CHAPTER 4

Surpassing Goals

A S A LEADER, it is important to motivate your teams to *surpass* goals rather than to merely *meet* them. Now, why would that be?

Well, first of all, when your team not only meets but also exceeds a goal, it boosts morale and job satisfaction throughout the team.

Second, surpassing a goal helps to foster a culture of continuous improvement, as it encourages the team to consistently strive for better and better results. They learn that it's not enough to settle for minimum expectations but that they should always be reaching a little farther, trying a little harder, and learning a little more.

Third, surpassing goals leads to improved performance and better outcomes for the entire organization. People don't generally strive for mediocrity, though they may settle for it if they lack the proper encouragement, support, and motivation. On the contrary, most people aspire to excel at what they do. Most people want to achieve great things and do their best. Surpassing goals reflects this desire for excellence, and it leads to both enhanced outcomes *and* a positive work environment.

So what can leaders do to create an environment where employees feel encouraged, inspired, and supported to surpass goals and always try to achieve more? In my experience, the single most important thing a leader can do is to create an environment of trust. The connection between trust and excellence may not be obvious, so let me explain.

According to a study in *Harvard Business Review*, people who have a high degree of trust in their leaders have 74 percent less stress, 106 percent more energy at work, and 50 percent higher productivity.[3] Clearly, trust plays a pivotal role in building stronger business relationships and more effective decision-making within teams.

When employees trust their leaders, they feel more comfortable sharing their thoughts and ideas, even if they disagree. This openness leads to better collaboration, more constructive dialogue, a diversity of perspectives, and greater problem-solving, as individuals become more willing to step outside their comfort zones and seek assistance from their colleagues.

In fact, dissenting views can often provide valuable insights that challenge assumptions and improve decision quality. As a business leader or director, you should be actively cultivating an environment of trust where all viewpoints are welcomed and sincerely considered. By acknowledging both the "glass-half-full" and "glass-half-empty" perspectives among team members, leaders can make more informed decisions and drive toward exceeding expectations rather than settling for mediocrity.

Moreover, trust increases motivation and engagement among employees. When there is a foundation of trust, employees become more invested in their work, which results in increased productivity and efficiency. High levels of trust lead to better quality work overall, which minimizes the need for revisions and additional support from coworkers. Ultimately, an environment of trust creates a healthy workplace where everyone feels valued and wants to contribute to surpassing goals.

On the other hand, a lack of trust will ultimately undermine morale and jeopardize goal attainment across the board in any organization. So, as a leader, it's your job to do everything you can to foster trust among team members and leaders.

When Trust Erodes

I have seen several scenarios over the course of my career where trust issues with leaders significantly impacted team performance. One common situation where this happens is during periods of reductions in force, which usually serve as a full reset of trust within the team. When multiple people are let go, it breeds insecurity among employees, leading to a lack of confidence in leadership directives.

As a director, it can be extremely challenging to rebuild trust postreduction, yet it's imperative that both frontline leaders and employees feel secure in their environment. Transparency is key in this process. Even if certain information is restricted due to confidentiality agreements, acknowledging these restrictions will contribute to a sense of honesty and accountability.

Two other trust-diminishing scenarios occur when leaders micromanage or prioritize personal goals over team objectives. These kinds of behaviors erode trust and undermine team morale, resulting in decreased performance and engagement. As a leader, recognize signs of micromanagement and take immediate action to address them. Signs of micromanagement include things like (1) a resistance to delegate work, (2) asking for frequent updates on even minor tasks, (3) discouraging independent thinking, (4) obsessing over details instead of the big picture, and (5) being really hard to satisfy.

If these things describe your approach to leadership, or the approach of the manager and leaders who are under you, then significant damage may already have been done to your team's trust. However, you can mitigate the damage and rebuild trust by coaching leaders, providing feedback on their leadership style, or demonstrating alternative leadership techniques. The sooner you start correcting this problem, the easier it will be to turn things around.

This is worth your time and attention. In fact, it's always worth the extra effort to rebuild trust, because trust is essential for maintaining high-performance teams. Whether navigating organizational changes or addressing leadership challenges, prioritizing trust-building efforts is absolutely necessary for achieving and surpassing organizational goals.

> Leadership is not about pushing what you want done but getting others to see the need to do so.
> **—STEPHANIE FEISS,**
> Sr. Director Network Operations

Creating a Culture of Performance

Leaders shape the culture and work environment of their teams. When they prioritize trust, honesty, and transparency, they create an atmosphere where team members feel comfortable sharing their ideas and collaborating regularly toward shared goals. Recognition and acknowledgment of team members' contributions further reinforce that trust within the team. Whether it's through verbal praise or formal recognition programs, acknowledging achievements motivates team members to work harder and take ownership of their tasks, further contributing to a sense of investment in both individual and team success.

Additionally, leaders who make a conscious effort to promote the growth and development of team members help instill confidence and competence in their roles. This encouragement enables team members to pursue various career paths and skill development opportunities, ultimately enhancing their overall performance and readiness for advancement. When team members have trust and confidence in their own abilities, they become more motivated to excel in their roles and contribute to the team's success.

In an environment where trust is prioritized, accomplishments are recognized, and growth opportunities are provided, a team will actively contribute to building a positive and thriving organizational culture that regularly meets and surpasses goals.

Motivation in the Growth Phase

During the growth phase of a company, investing in your team becomes even more important. In this period of time in a company's life, leaders must learn the delicate balance between seeing the glass half full and half empty, evaluating what's working and what's not. This is when it's more important than ever to foster an environment of celebration and acknowledgment, where hard work is recognized, and achievements are celebrated collectively.

The journey of team building involves various strategies, from conducting skip-level meetings to ensure every voice is heard, to emphasizing collaboration and communication across all layers of leadership. However, amid the quest for success, there lies a cautionary tale of ineffective leadership that could jeopardize the very fabric of trust within a team.

One common mistake I've observed in the real world is when leaders prioritize their personal goals over the collective success of the team. This often manifests in setting unrealistic targets driven solely by personal ambitions, which creates an authoritarian environment where results are demanded at any cost.

While such an approach may yield short-term gains, it comes at the expense of long-term trust and morale within the team. Employees may deliver the desired results, but the bridges burned in the process can have lasting repercussions on the team's cohesion and productivity.

As a leader, you need to strike a balance between driving performance and nurturing a supportive work environment. Building trust takes time and effort, and it's a fragile element that can be easily shattered by short-sighted leadership practices.

Effective leadership entails not only achieving and surpassing targets but also fostering an atmosphere where individuals feel valued, heard, and empowered. That means recognizing the contributions of each team member and cultivating a culture of collaboration and mutual respect.

As a leader, you have to do more than just meet performance metrics. To truly motivate and inspire your team, you need empathy, integrity, and a commitment to long-term success. By prioritizing the well-being and growth of your team members, you lay the foundation for sustainable success and foster a culture where everyone thrives.

The growth and development of people is the highest calling of leadership.

—HARVEY S. FIRESTONE

CHAPTER 5

Building Your Technical Talent Pool

A LEADER NEEDS TO have a good pool of technical talent at all times, especially in an ever-evolving organization, so you always have people who can bring in-depth technical expertise to help your business stay competitive. New talent is also going to help you stay adaptable as the technological landscape changes.

This is particularly important in my industry, telecommunications, because we are constantly dealing with system upgrades and new widgets of one kind or another. Any organization in this industry needs to maintain a pool of people with the technical expertise to handle whatever new thing comes along, whether it's entirely new technology or the same technology with a different look and feel.

From an innovation perspective, it's incredibly important to tap into your pool of technical talent for fresh ideas. New people often bring novel and inventive ideas that can propel the organization forward and help keep you at the forefront of progress. Fresh perspectives from outside the company can challenge the status quo and push everyone to reconsider their current approach. In my experience, I've found this to be the primary driver of innovation.

On the other hand, there's also the kind of innovation born out of necessity, particularly when your team is faced with an overwhelming workload. In such situations, people are often compelled to innovate solutions in order to mitigate the burden, and those solutions often end up enhancing overall efficiency. However, this type of innovation doesn't necessarily come solely from a technical standpoint; it arises from the need to adapt and overcome all kinds of challenges (technical and otherwise) in the workplace.

Finally, it's important to cultivate a strong pool of technical talent within the organization for succession planning as well so there's always a clear idea of what comes next and where the organization can evolve. The idea behind this approach is to minimize the risks associated with employee turnover. Even if attrition rates are ideally low, say 2 percent or less, it's inevitable that some talent will depart. In such situations, you need to have a succession plan in place that identifies who is prepared and best suited to step up and fill any vacated roles.

Failing to Maintain a Pool of Talent

While these are all positive reasons to maintain a pool of technical talent, there are also some distinct dangers that come from not doing so. There are three dangers in particular.

- Increased Risk
- Decreased Innovation
- It Becomes Difficult to Scale

Let's look at each of these.

Increased Risk

If you don't maintain a good pool of technical talent, you increase the risk of experiencing downtimes and outages. For an operations director like me, this is the biggest and most significant danger. After all, if you don't have the right skillset to fix a problem, customers could be impacted.

In my industry, that might mean someone can't make a 911 call while sitting on the side of the road because the exact right person isn't available to fix whatever the problem might be. Or maybe a customer can't use their Uber app at 2 o'clock in the morning because of a system outage, and they are standing on the sidewalk, intoxicated. These kinds of scenarios should keep any leader awake at night.

It doesn't matter if the problem is internal or external. You must have the right people with the right skill set available 24/7 who can fix problems and make certain that these kinds of customer scenarios don't happen. Depending on your industry, lives might be at stake. But at the very least, your customer relationships and company reputation are at stake.

Look, attrition happens. It's unavoidable. Sooner or later, you're going to lose some of your best talents to other opportunities or life circumstances, and all of the time and resources you've invested in them won't matter because they won't be around to fix your problems. And unless you have a good pool of talent to draw from in order to fill those gaps, you're going to have additional downtime and outages. Over time, this can become a downward spiral of worsening problems, so don't let it start to happen in the first place.

Decreased Innovation

Without a good pool of technical talent, it becomes a struggle just to keep up with the lead technologies and innovations in your industry. I have seen this quite a lot over the years, the most recent example being automation. Over time, automation became deep learning, deep learning became machine learning, and finally we wound up with what we call AI (artificial intelligence). We'll talk about these three different phases of AI in a later chapter.

The point is, you need to have innovative people who can think outside of the box, who can move beyond the old mindset that says, "This is how we've always done it," and instead says, "We can do this better. We can leverage this new technology to do what we need better, faster, and safer." If you don't have people like that, it puts you at a competitive disadvantage.

This might not even be external competition with other businesses. Maybe it's internal. Sometimes teams and departments within a business can be highly competitive with each other: engineering versus marketing versus sales. If one department is falling behind another because of a lack of technical talent, that can become a hindrance to collaboration.

Still, between the two, the bigger risk is definitely external competition. If other companies are finding disruptive ways to leverage technology, and you don't have the technical talent on your own team to keep up, then you're going to have a difficult time beating them in the market.

Difficulty Scaling

If you're not careful about maintaining your pool of technical talent, it's only going to become harder as your company grows. As you get bigger, you're going to struggle even more to bring on new technical talent quickly enough, train them, and get them set up. Having a succession plan for people who leave will only get more difficult, and it's a problem that's going to compound.

Soon, you'll have this growing void, with tumbleweeds instead of talent, which will eventually bring your growth to a complete standstill since your team can no longer keep up with the demands of the business.

Dealing with the Void

I've had to deal with a few voids in talents during my time as a leader. In fact, one of them happened recently. We went through a reduction of force and lost the people who handled software upgrades, integrating new tools, and guaranteed compliance and security within the business.

This kind of work demands meticulous attention. Our telecommunications company had its own software team to manage these updates, just like Microsoft or Apple. However, during the reduction in force, this talent exited the business.

Consequently, we found ourselves relying on external vendors to fill the gap, which led to significant financial outlays. Specifically, we had to pay a vendor approximately $97,000 to compensate for the lost talents' absence. This reliance on third-party support prevented us from self-performing essential tasks, which ultimately became a big problem, an even bigger expense, and a constant source of frustration.

But this is the kind of challenge you face when you lack a robust talent pool. You can't just fill the void overnight. Training new personnel takes time, and meanwhile, the work continues to demand attention. The business's needs persist, regardless of internal restructuring or personnel changes. And those needs are only magnified when you're considering opportunities for growth and expansion.

As another example, I was with a company called Clearwire back in the day. At that time, it was a small startup, but we were growing so fast that we couldn't hire people and teach them quickly enough to meet our needs. We had some new equipment installed, powered up, and ready for customers to use, but we couldn't bring it online for months because we didn't have people who could get in there, test it, and ensure that it was stable.

We didn't have anyone to answer the questions: Does it have resiliency? Can it fail over? Can it do all the enterprise-grade things that we've purchased? And so it was running, but no customers could connect to it, and we had no way to come up with new tools or creative approaches to make it magically work behind the scenes. We just didn't have a strong pool of technical talent that could expand beyond their existing work volumes. And even if we brought people on board, we couldn't teach them fast enough to help us scale.

These are two sides of the same coin. You can grow so quickly that you can't get new people in place fast enough, or you can go through a reduction and, if you're not incredibly careful about what talent you're maintaining, you could find yourself with a void, lacking certain skill sets in your technical talent pool.

> Everyone is replaceable and many things can trigger the need for new leadership. It could be a retirement, a resignation, a personal situation, or a performance issue. Identify future leaders based on current performance and the potential to grow. Provide the training, mentorship, and exposure needed to help grow people into more responsibility, so that you always have a bench ready to rotate.
>
> **—JOE MEYER,**
> VP of Network Operations

Learning and Development Opportunities

We've talked about the many problems that happen when you don't maintain a pool of technical talent, but the truth is, nobody wants to have a void in their workforce. Nobody wants there to be missing skill sets, whether it happens as a result of things like growth, reduction in force, or moving people on.

So what can you do to build and maintain a pool of technical talent at all times and in every growth stage of your company? I believe the most important thing a leader can do is to offer people learning and development opportunities. You have to invest in your staff, especially when it comes to technical resources. If a team member wants to get some new technical certification, help them get it. Pay for the certification. If you're a director, budget for it and make sure you have money sitting in a reserve to fund such things.

Technical talent is always looking for opportunities to grow and develop their skills. They want to be on the cutting edge of whatever they're working on. So provide them with training. Pay for the programs and workshops that will improve their skill set. Allow them to attend conferences that will help them stay up to date on what's new and what's coming in the near future.

I mention conferences specifically because I know a lot of directors approach conferences with a conviction that they don't add value to the business. After all, conferences, with a few exceptions, don't give people certification at the end. But I see it very differently. In fact, conferences have proved to be one of the most valuable investments I've made, and they have provided consistent and significant returns year after year.

There's a perception in my industry that if you send people to a conference, you're sending them to party for three to five days, especially if the conference is in some exciting place like Las Vegas. I would argue that you're actually fostering collaboration. Your team members are going to meet professionals from various fields and gain insight into how other businesses operate. They will also establish connections within vendor networks, who can provide valuable support when needed, even at odd hours.

Furthermore, conferences typically offer free training sessions that are aimed at promoting new products or technologies. While these may seem like sales pitches, technical experts can still discern valuable insights from them and learn how different components integrate and function. This knowledge sharpens their skills and keeps them abreast of the latest developments, which they can then share with the rest of the team upon their return.

Are conferences worth the cost? I believe so. Let's say it costs about a thousand dollars per person to send someone to a conference. If you send three team members, you will spend $3,000. Is that too much? Well, in my opinion, you can't purchase $3,000 worth of training that provides all of the same benefits. Even a certification, which will probably be priced closer to $30,000, doesn't offer the same advantages because it's a solo journey for one individual. A conference, however, is a learning opportunity with a unique social element.

From conferences and classes to workshops and certification courses, all of these offer you significant returns on your investment by increasing and improving the skill sets of your team members, fostering collaboration, and creating connections, so I encourage you to provide your team with a variety of learning and development opportunities.

> Leaders are not those with the most followers,
> they are the ones who create the most leaders.
> **—ANGEL MARCHAND,**
> Sr. Director Network Operations

Elements of a Positive Work Environment

While continuous learning ensures that your team remains competitive and capable of meeting the evolving demands of the business landscape, it's just as important to foster a positive work environment. By "positive," I'm talking about a work environment that promotes inclusivity and allows individuals to support each other. This kind of collaborative atmosphere not only aids in talent retention but also cultivates a strong technical talent pool capable of addressing diverse challenges.

Alongside this, providing flexible work schedules, acknowledging achievements, and offering competitive compensation and benefits are also vitally important. It's imperative for directors to engage with HR and advocate for their teams to guarantee competitive pay scales across the industry. Failure to do so risks losing your best technical talent to better-paying opportunities elsewhere, regardless of how positive your workplace environment may be.

Remember, people are largely motivated by financial incentives, and if they discover the potential for a significantly higher salary somewhere else, they may seek out those opportunities, no matter what kind of culture you've created for them. Therefore, as a leader, you need to actively liaise with HR professionals and leverage their influence to uphold competitive pay standards so you retain valuable technical talent.

Finally, technical talent thrives in an environment where they can freely experiment and take risks. Give them the latitude to innovate, and you will foster creativity and growth, which are essential elements in advancing technical expertise. Without the opportunity to take risks, innovation stagnates, and individuals become less inclined to push boundaries or explore new ideas. Over time, they lose enthusiasm for the work they're doing, and they may start looking for more exciting opportunities elsewhere.

Of course, you have to maintain a balance in order to make sure that experimentation occurs within controlled environments such as labs rather than in production settings where customer satisfaction could be compromised. The goal isn't to break things but to encourage innovation while maintaining operational stability.

Just remember, if you're a director or vice president, it's your responsibility to create a culture that values and encourages innovation. This may involve implementing processes that facilitate experimentation, providing resources for exploration, or actively encouraging employees to propose and develop new ideas.

Investing in the latest technologies for your team to explore will not only enhance their skills but also prepare them to tackle production issues with confidence and proficiency. By nurturing a culture of innovation, you empower your technical talent to continuously learn and adapt, ultimately benefiting both the individual and the organization as a whole.

The Impact of New Talent

Maybe all of this sounds like a lot of work. Paying for certification and conferences, promoting inclusivity, ensuring competitive compensation, encouraging a culture of innovation, and providing your team with the latest technologies? That sure sounds like a lot, and what are you going to get for all of that? Well, you're going to get a steady pool of innovative, positive, and committed technical talent that can solve problems faster and stay ahead of the curve.

I'll share a couple of examples from my own experience. In both instances, recent college graduates came on board and made a quick impact on the company. College graduates often bring a fresh perspective to the table, and it's always refreshing to see their unique approaches. It's not always perfect, and sometimes they have a bit of a learning curve because of their youthfulness, but their presence almost always compels people to consider things from different angles.

New talent doesn't necessarily come with years of experience, but they bring a foundation of skills that are distinct from the seasoned professionals. When they join the team, they often introduce the latest technologies and approaches that are aimed at achieving maximum efficiency. It has been interesting to observe how their strategies often seem to prioritize achieving goals with minimal effort. I wonder if this mindset is something instilled during their college years, perhaps driven by a desire to excel in exams.

Whatever the case, in my experience, these newcomers frequently propose innovative solutions, whether that means utilizing specific new technologies or implementing unconventional marketing tactics. They're not afraid to leverage tools like PowerPoint in ways that others might not have considered. Their ability to think outside the box has been instrumental in several situations where swift action was needed to overcome challenges.

Both of these stories are about dealing with network outages.

In the first instance, we were grappling with a persistent issue at one of our cell sites for months. Like clockwork, every day at 8:00 AM and 5:00 PM, the site would go down for about five minutes. Despite our best efforts, we couldn't pinpoint the cause. Although we weren't experts in cell sites—we primarily focused on the core—we were all-hands-on-deck trying to resolve the issue. Then, a new college graduate joined our team and suggested taking a step back to reassess the situation.

This fresh perspective led him to open Google Maps, where he made a surprising discovery. He noticed a pattern: a line of milk trucks regularly formed on the highway precisely at 8:00 AM and 5:00 PM. These trucks obstructed the microwave shot crucial for the cell site's operation. As they unloaded their deliveries, the signal was disrupted, which caused the site to go down temporarily. Once the trucks left, the signal restored itself, almost as if by magic.

It was a revelation. Despite the complexity of our troubleshooting efforts, the solution was remarkably simple. None of us had considered the possibility of external interference. We had overlooked the basic principle of cause and effect. It took a newcomer, armed with nothing but Google Maps and a fresh perspective, to uncover the root cause of our problem. In retrospect, it seemed obvious, but in the midst of our frustration, it had eluded us. This experience taught us the value of simplicity and the importance of looking at problems from all angles, no matter how unconventional they may seem.

In the second instance, we encountered a perplexing database issue that manifested intermittently, causing occasional errors that mysteriously self-corrected. Despite investing significant time and effort into the investigation, the root cause eluded us. Again, a recent college graduate joined our team and brought a fresh perspective to the table.

This new recruit possessed expertise in Python scripting, but what stood out was his innovative approach to problem-solving. Drawing from his experience in an engineering class, he proposed building a model to analyze the database's behavior. We set up a test environment and began feeding data into the model. To our astonishment, we discovered that another system was sending erroneous commands to the database, causing it to drop connections as instructed.

It was another revelation that highlighted the power of simplicity in problem-solving. Despite the complexity of our network infrastructure, the solution was surprisingly straightforward. This experience served as a reminder that sometimes the most intricate issues have simple solutions that elude even the most technically adept individuals. We were so focused on delving into the technical complexity that we overlooked the straightforward solution right in front of us.

Invest in Your Team

New people bring in new fresh ideas. That's another reason to make sure you always have a talent pool that contains everyone from junior engineers to senior engineers, and then you have to give them a culture where they can innovate and explore.

As a leader, I encourage you to invest in your team. Frontline leaders should be spending a lot of time with their team to make sure they have what they need. Directors should aim for a 50/50 split, so they spend about half of their time with the team.

Create a positive culture where your team members can collaborate and innovate. Provide them with opportunities to learn and grow. Set aside money for workshops, classes, certification courses, and, yes, conferences. The returns you get for all of this will be a pool of talented people with a broad skill set to meet all of your technical needs.

If you always do what you've always done, you'll always get what you've always got.

—ANONYMOUS

CHAPTER 6

Innovation versus Stability

I N LEADERSHIP, THERE'S a delicate balancing act that emerges, often swinging back and forth like a pendulum, between the realms of innovation and stability, especially in technical operations. This delicate dance is generally driven by three primary considerations: (1) managing risk, (2) efficiently utilizing resources, and (3) adeptly responding to evolving demands.

First, innovation inherently involves taking risks, but innovative ventures do not always yield the desired outcome. Leaders must meticulously assess the potential consequences of these risks against the promised rewards, while at the same time safeguarding the stability of their network. This requires a keen eye for discerning the value proposition of innovation amid inherent uncertainties.

Second, leaders have to carefully manage their resources. Embracing innovation often requires substantial investments, both in terms of capital and human resources. Operational expenditures and the allocation of additional resources also factor into the equation. Thus, leaders must navigate a tricky path between budgetary constraints and the imperative to foster innovation.

Third, the need to respond to changing demands looms large in many industries. In the dynamic landscape of business, flux is constant, and that demands agility and responsiveness from leaders. Adapting to shifting customer needs and market dynamics while simultaneously upholding network stability presents a formidable challenge. Effective leadership must somehow learn how to swiftly pivot in response to emerging trends and demands, while at the same time ensuring that the integrity of their network remains uncompromised. This is no easy feat, not even for the most experienced leaders!

Clearly, striking a balance between innovation and stability demands a nuanced approach, one characterized by smart risk management, resource optimization, and agile responsiveness. Amid the constant changes of the business landscape, maintaining a steadfast commitment to customer-centricity and network integrity is of the utmost importance. Somehow, leaders must skillfully confront the tensions inherent in this dual mandate in order to make certain that innovation propels growth while stability safeguards continuity.

Too Much Innovation

Swinging too far toward innovation can spell trouble for the stability of a network and existing systems. While innovation is undeniably important for staying ahead of the curve and enhancing your efficiency, an excessive focus on it can introduce too much complexity and jeopardize reliability. These two objectives often clash, but somehow leaders have to weigh the respective merits and the potential impacts of each one before implementing any new strategies or technologies into a network.

In my experience, it's not uncommon for leaders to become overly enamored with innovation to the detriment of stability. As an example, consider the current landscape of artificial intelligence (AI). Many leaders are eager to harness the potential of AI, but they must tread carefully and understand the potential risks.

Despite the touted benefits of AI in revolutionizing workforce efficiency and accelerating speed-to-market, there are some potential pitfalls. After all, AI may not consistently provide the desired or intended responses or meet customer demands. Failing to account for this can lead to misguided expectations and operational inefficiencies.

Quite frankly, there is a stark difference between an AI-*enabled* workforce and an AI workforce. An AI-enabled workforce empowers employees with enhanced access to information which facilitates more informed decision-making. However, ultimate control remains in human hands, ensuring a balance between technological augmentation and human judgment. On the other hand, an AI workforce surrenders decision-making authority to automated systems, potentially compromising network stability and reliability.

Unfortunately, many leaders, enticed by the promise of AI, have veered too far into the realm of automation and overlooked the critical importance of stability. Despite initial successes, these ventures often falter when confronted with unforeseen challenges. It's an all-too-common scenario these days, and it's one more reason why the allure of cutting-edge technologies must be tempered by a realistic assessment of their implications. Leaders must recognize that sustainable progress hinges upon a sensible integration of innovation and stability.

Too Much Stability

On the other hand, sometimes a leader veers excessively toward stability, and in the process largely, or entirely, abandons innovation. This approach carries the risk of stagnation, as opportunities for improvement and advancement are overlooked or intentionally ignored.

An overly cautious stance, driven by a fear of risk, often proves detrimental to progress. Leaders must realize that a reluctance to embrace change can result in their companies falling behind competitors who are more adept at seizing opportunities and adapting to evolving landscapes.

If you fail to innovate, you may be outpaced and ultimately left behind in the competitive arena. Of course, it is imperative to conduct thorough risk assessments and weigh the potential benefits of any proposed changes. Informed decision-making lies at the heart of striking the right balance between stability and innovation. While prudence is necessary, leaning too heavily toward network stability risks sacrificing long-term viability and relevance. In essence, leaders must strive to create a delicate equilibrium so that they remain competitive and future-proof.

In my industry, I've always worked on the wireless technical side. But a few decades ago, leaders on the wireline side of the industry, the home telephone network companies, failed to invest in wireless technology because they were risk averse. They considered wireless technology too expensive, too risky, and it wasn't always available at the time due to limited coverage.

From the early '90s through the early 2000s, the wireline companies continued to resist embracing wireless innovation because they didn't understand what it could become. Eventually, they got left behind, and when wireless technology took over the world, many of those companies found that their organizations were untrained and ill-prepared for the change. They were not in a position to grow with wireless technology, so customers found themselves having to make the unpleasant choice of either making calls on their cell phones *or* making a call on their wired home telephone—their home telephone could not do both.

These companies sought stability and resisted innovation for so long that they weren't able to take advantage of the rise of wireless technology when it began to dominate the market. Meanwhile, over in the wireless space, we were doing amazing things with a fraction of the resources that the home telephone teams had.

Over time, having a cell phone became the new norm, and consumers started turning off their home phones to use cell phones exclusively. The home telephone side of the industry missed out because leaders hadn't taken those early innovative leaps.

But why did they resist embracing the change for so long? Why did they fail to leverage all of the new tools, resources, and technology that were becoming available? Because they believed that stability was more important than investing in what they saw as risky trends and new technology.

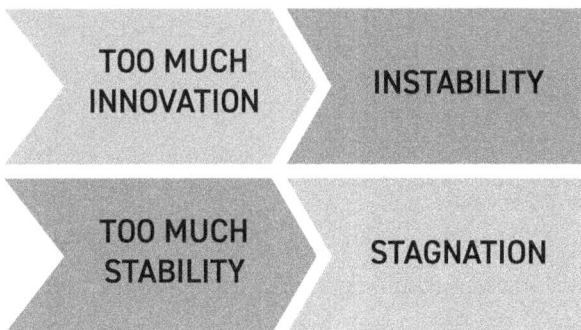

TOO MUCH INNOVATION	INSTABILITY
TOO MUCH STABILITY	STAGNATION

Tips for Maintaining Balance

So how can you maintain the delicate balance between stability and innovation? How do you embrace important changes and new technology without swinging so widely that you jeopardize your relationship with customers or the demands of the current market? It's not always an easy balance to maintain. However, I recommend the five following tactics, some of which might surprise you.

- Prioritize Tasks
- Time Management
- Communication
- Take Breaks
- Continuous Learning

Let's take a look at each one.

Prioritize Tasks
When you prioritize tasks, you are essentially making a list of all the tasks that need to be accomplished and prioritizing them based on their level of importance. Doing this clarifies which tasks are absolutely critical, so you can focus on them and complete them on time. Otherwise, important tasks are liable to be overlooked, and you might lose sight of foundational aspects of your business while innovation gets all of your time and attention.

Time Management
Effective time management is also vitally important for maintaining balance between stability and innovation. Without adept time management skills, both on an individual and team level, achieving

this balance becomes a formidable challenge. Meticulously allocate time for each task and adhere to a structured schedule. This guarantees that attention is given to both stability and innovation in equal measure, which will optimize productivity and progress.

A key aspect of effective time management is the avoidance of multitasking. While multitasking may seem like a shortcut to efficiency, my experience has taught me otherwise. Engaging in multitasking can lead to heightened stress levels and eventual burnout among staff members. Though it may yield short-term gains, its long-term consequences are detrimental. Steer clear of multitasking and instead focus on prioritizing tasks and allocating dedicated time to each, fostering a sustainable and balanced approach to work.

Communication

Clear communication from leaders plays a pivotal role in upholding the delicate balance between stability and innovation within your business. By fostering open lines of communication with your teams, other business units, and even customers, you lay the foundation for proactive problem anticipation and resolution. It's through this constant exchange that problems, which often manifest when new and innovative ideas are implemented, are revealed and addressed in a timely manner.

Maintaining transparent communication channels enables you to embrace challenges with a proactive mindset and turn problems into opportunities. Through open communication, you gain additional foresight into emerging trends and potential obstacles, which will empower you to navigate the business landscape with confidence and agility. Thus, effective communication serves as a linchpin in fostering a culture of adaptability and innovation within your organization.

Take Breaks

It's important to encourage breaks for both yourself and your team, but it goes beyond simply stepping away for a moment. It's also about ensuring that your staff takes breaks from their usual routines. If your team is constantly immersed in project after project without variation, then it's time for a change.

Give them downtime and opportunities for creativity and self-investment. Allow for flexibility in schedules, provide training sessions, and promote personal development. All of these things will contribute to maintaining balance.

Your senior leadership needs to understand the significance of taking breaks. Failure to recognize this can result in your staff seeking out other environments where their growth and well-being are prioritized.

By acknowledging the need for breaks and investing in your team's personal and professional development, you promote a culture that values and supports its members. This approach not only benefits individuals but also contributes to a more dynamic and resilient organization as a whole. Make sure breaks are integrated into the work routine because they will contribute to a healthy and productive workplace environment.

Continuous Learning

Finally, continuous learning stands as a cornerstone—not just for leaders, but for the entire organization—to maintaining a competitive edge in today's rapidly evolving business and technology landscape. Leaders have to stay abreast of the latest trends and technologies if they want to stay ahead of the curve.

While topics like artificial intelligence may dominate discussions now, the future holds different innovations, some we haven't yet begun to imagine, so you need to constantly update your understanding of emerging concepts. Attend conferences and invest in educational opportunities, both for yourself as well as your teams, because they will yield significant benefits.

However, as we said before, continuous learning is not limited to conferences alone. Workshops, training sessions, and collaboration with third parties all contribute to a comprehensive understanding of industry trends. Encourage your team's innovation and idea generation so your organization remains agile and forward-thinking.

The benefits of continuous learning extend beyond professional growth; they also help your people to maintain a healthy balance between work and personal life. When you invest in your employees' well-being, both professionally and personally, you instill a sense of empowerment and resilience, help them avoid getting burned out, and, yes, strike a balance between stability and innovation.

The result of all of this is going to be increased productivity and a better work-life balance for all involved. Ultimately, prioritizing continuous learning ensures that both individuals and the organization as a whole thrive in an ever-changing environment.

> The definitions of innovation and stability make them appear to be natural enemies. However, they are actually close partners. We must continuously explore improvements to provide, or preserve, the stability of the goods and services customers demand. Otherwise, we might all still be huddled around a smoky wood fire in a cave, lamenting over how the loin cloth chafes.
>
> **—KEITH MATHIES,**
> VP of Network

Every Employee Can Be Innovative

Let me share a real-life scenario that demonstrates the delicate balance between stability and innovation. It taught me a valuable lesson: every employee has the potential for innovation. When an employee brings forth an innovative idea, it's important to invest in them, even if it means temporarily reassigning them from their usual role to explore new avenues.

In this instance, a technician presented a process improvement idea. He mentioned that if he had access to specific information when addressing certain ongoing challenges, he would significantly enhance his problem-solving capabilities. I saw merit in his suggestion, so I encouraged collaboration between different departments by creating a small, agile team—a "tiger team," if you will—to work on implementing the technician's idea.

As the project unfolded, the technician stepped out of his usual routine, and as a result, he gained exposure to different aspects of the organization. Meanwhile, other departments gained insights into the challenges faced by their colleagues. This collaborative effort culminated in the development of a streamlined solution. Within just three months, we consolidated data from multiple sources into a single platform, empowering our technicians to resolve issues in a fraction of the time it previously took.

This experience demonstrates what I believe to be the essence of leadership: leveraging resources across teams and forging partnerships to drive innovation. As a junior executive, I learned that effective leadership extends beyond organizational boundaries and silos. Our collaborative approach not only enhanced productivity but also fostered a culture of innovation and continuous improvement—a testament to the power of teamwork and strategic partnerships.

That technician got to learn about automation. He learned about databasing and how tools actually work—and not just how you log into a tool but the backend of those tools. At the same time, the other groups got to learn the frontline experience and the real-world implications of various challenges we faced. This teamwork led to innovation, while at the same time helping maintain network stability by enabling us to fix issues faster—a perfect example of balancing innovation and stability.

By failing to prepare, you are preparing to fail.

—BENJAMIN FRANKLIN

CHAPTER 7

Handling Crises and Network Outages

OW YOU RESPOND to a crisis is the truest test of your leadership abilities. I've personally witnessed a number of instances where leaders handling a crisis poorly led to a truly detrimental outcome. This is especially true when you're dealing with a network outage, which is one of the most common challenges in my industry.

In fact, there are generally four kinds of mistakes I've witnessed in how leaders navigate these situations. These mistakes include (1) a lack of communication, (2) a tendency to blame others, (3) the absence of a concrete plan, and (4) a failure to learn from past experiences. Each of these pitfalls presents significant challenges and hinders the effective resolution of a crisis (especially a network crisis).

First, let's discuss the issue of communication. This is perhaps the most common mistake I've seen leaders make during network crises. They fail to communicate clearly about what has happened, how it's being dealt with, or what comes next. They may lack empathy for their employees when they communicate, or they may avoid saying anything at all because they don't want to be the bearers of bad news. But effective communication with your team is especially important during difficult times, yet it's shockingly common for leaders to struggle in this area.

In fact, the root cause of many crises is usually either a skill or communication gap, whether it's nontechnical personnel attempting to address technical issues or leaders tackling process problems. A lack of effective communication creates confusion and delays in resolving the crisis, which makes the problem all the worse.

Second, some leaders have a bad habit of blaming other people when things go wrong. To be fair, this is a self-protection skill we all learn as children. When little kids get caught with their hands in the cookie jar, they instinctively point the finger at brother or sister in a desperate attempt to avoid punishment. We say things like, "He made me do it!" Unfortunately, we often continue to do this well into adulthood, and even bring this tendency to our roles as leaders.

I've seen far too many leaders who are quick to point fingers at different business units or other individuals instead of taking responsibility themselves for whatever the problem happens to be. This blame shifting not only creates a toxic work environment but also erodes morale. Leaders who do this undermine the trust and collaborative spirit they may have worked hard to build (as we discussed in previous chapters) and create barriers among team members. A *senior* leader who indulges in this behavior reflects poorly on the entire team and exacerbates the crisis rather than solving or alleviating it.

Third, the absence of a comprehensive plan for dealing with a crisis intensifies and adds to the challenges. Sometimes, leaders fail to create a comprehensive plan for crisis management because they believe the chances of a crisis happening are extremely low, or maybe they just don't want to think about worst-case scenarios. However, without a plan, the aftermath of a crisis is almost always far worse and much harder to overcome.

Again, this is particularly true when dealing with a network outage, especially in a large-scale scenario like a natural disaster. For example, when a hurricane ravaged Puerto Rico some years ago, inadequate planning resulted in logistical nightmares and long delays in delivering essential supplies and aid to suffering people. A lack of preparedness not only prolongs a crisis but also contributes to network instability, which negatively affects everyone involved and makes a resolution even more difficult.

Finally, the most avoidable, yet impactful, mistake leaders make is failing to learn from past experiences. Leaders who fail to conduct postmortems and glean insights from previous crises are bound to repeat the same mistakes. As the famous saying goes, "Those who fail to learn from history are doomed to repeat it."

A wise leader analyzes each incident thoroughly so they can identify areas of needed improvement and document lessons learned to prevent them from happening again. When you bypass this important step, you and your team remain trapped in a cycle of avoidable errors which, again, perpetuate network instability and undermine your overall effectiveness.

So effectively managing network crises requires four things:

- Proactive Communication
- Accountability

- Meticulous Planning
- A Commitment to Continuous Improvement.

By addressing these four key areas, you will be able to navigate crises more adeptly and strengthen your team against future challenges.

> One of the key measures of a leader is how they show up and support their peers, teams, and customers during a crisis.
>
> **—BRIAN KING,**
> CIO and COO of Technology

The Impact of Poor Crisis Management

Getting these four things right is extremely important because poor crisis management has negative impacts on your team's culture and performance and on the company as a whole. The consequences can be broad and long-ranging. Mishandling a network crisis, for example, affects not only the technical aspects of your company but also deeply influences organizational dynamics and your company's reputation in the marketplace. Let's look at these negative outcomes a little closer so you understand why this issue is so important.

For starters, ineffective crisis management can severely damage your team's morale and their confidence in your leadership. That, in turn, can lead to a decrease in productivity, and the resulting stress and tension within the team can further deteriorate the organizational culture, creating a hostile or demotivated work environment.

Moreover, prolonged network outages will inflict reputational damage on your company. If customers experience disruptions in essential services like phone calls, data usage, or messaging because of network failures, it's going to tarnish their perception of your entire company. That negative perception will eventually translate into a loss of customers and revenue, so it's a significant threat to your company's sustainability and growth—not something to take lightly!

If you're a network operations director like me, it's your responsibility to handle crises effectively so you can mitigate these negative impacts on your team culture and company reputation. It's also your job to protect your team's cohesion and the company's standing in the market.

With that in mind, let's look at three strategies for handling crises in general, and network outages in particular. There are three key tips I'd like to highlight:

1) Have a Solid Plan in Place

You need to have a solid plan in place *before* a crisis strikes. Prepare well-defined plans for various crisis scenarios so your team will be equipped to respond swiftly and effectively when an outage occurs. Your plans should outline the necessary steps, identify the teams involved, allocate responsibilities, and establish communication protocols to keep stakeholders informed.

2) Act Quickly and Decisively

When a crisis strikes, you need to act quickly and decisively. Swift action can help contain the damage and expedite the resolution process. Be ready to make informed decisions promptly, mobilize resources efficiently, and coordinate efforts to minimize downtime and mitigate disruptions.

While having a structured plan is essential, it's equally vital to empower your teams to act. This empowerment should be ingrained into the plan itself. Every second counts, so make sure you have the right team in place and ready to go. Are they trained and equipped to handle such situations? Do they possess the autonomy to make on-the-spot decisions?

Team members should already know they have the authority to take necessary actions without constantly seeking approval from higher-ups. Whether it's rebooting equipment or redirecting traffic in a data center, they should feel empowered to act decisively.

This approach fosters self-sufficiency among team members and enables them to prevent crises from getting worse. It's part of their role to step up during such critical moments, just as much as it is for a leader. By entrusting them with decision-making authority and fostering a culture of empowerment, the team can effectively navigate crises, mitigating their impact and ensuring swift resolution.

3) Learn from Past Experience

We touched on this already, but it's worth another mention. You will get better at handling crises if you learn from past experiences. Continuous improvement is incredibly important! I recommend conducting after-action reviews, or postmortems, after each crisis so your team can reflect on what worked well and what could be improved. Analyze both what went wrong and what went right. As Henry Ford put it, "The only real mistake is the one from which we learn nothing."

By identifying lessons learned and implementing corrective measures, you can improve your team's crisis response capabilities and prevent similar issues in the future. During the postmortem, it's important to meticulously document your findings and track them over time. Whether the issue stemmed from insufficient information, a lack of resilience, inadequate capacity, or any other reason, each lesson learned should be carefully noted. This allows for a comprehensive understanding of the root causes and necessary corrective actions.

Some solutions may be relatively straightforward and require immediate implementation, such as investing in additional resources or updating tools. Others may necessitate longer-term strategies, such as infrastructure improvements or capacity expansions. Regardless, the key is to actively address each identified issue and work toward resolution.

Failing to learn from past experiences and neglecting to track progress toward improvement perpetuates a cycle of recurrent crises. However, by leveraging insights gained from postmortems and taking proactive measures to address underlying issues, your organization can break free from this cycle and build resilience against future challenges.

By integrating these three strategies—(1) having a solid plan in place for dealing with various kinds of crises, (2) acting quickly and decisively when a crisis hits, (3) learning from past experiences—into your crisis management approach, you will develop a resilient team culture and safeguard your company's reputation in the face of all manager of challenges. In my experience, these three things are the pillars of successful crisis management in network operations, but they certainly apply more broadly to other areas.

> It is most important that an executive display a calm, logical, and fact-based demeanor during a crisis. Approach different levels of crises differently, depending on the broader picture and risk level. Provide guidance, influence, and resources to those solving the problems, but don't get in the way of the experts. Give them air cover with higher-level leadership, customers, and stakeholders so they can work the issue using their experience and technical knowledge to triage and problem-solve.
>
> **—JOE MEYER,**
> VP of Network Operations

My Approach to Crisis Management

I have learned these crisis management strategies the hard way—while confronting real-life challenges with my team. For example, I've dealt with many significant outages over the years, but there's one particular instance that comes to mind. It occurred years ago when I was working with a previous company in Burbank.

One day, we found ourselves dealing with a DDoS attack that effectively isolated an entire data center by locking up the firewalls, thus halting customer data traffic flow. What we learned from this incident was the importance of automatic route protections, which we didn't have at the time. Ideally, our traffic should have automatically shifted away from the affected data center to other data centers in Phoenix and Anaheim. However, since that wasn't the case, we had to manually reroute traffic and block the sources of the DDoS attack before redirecting it.

Breaking down the problem step by step, we managed to resolve it within forty-seven minutes from initial awareness to complete resolution. This involved blocking the DDoS vectors and then manually rerouting traffic but also implementing automatic route adjustments and additional DDoS protections for future incidents.

Afterward, we documented our findings and solutions and compiled them into a concise report. I use a specific template for this kind of documentation, which is categorized into *customer impact*, *summary of knowledge*, and *actions taken*. This standardized approach provides clear communication for both executives and stakeholders during a crisis and becomes a valuable reference during postmortems.

This technique, honed over fifteen years of experience, remains a cornerstone of my crisis management strategy. By adhering to this approach, I can effectively communicate the situation, actions taken, and lessons learned, which makes it easier for us to immediately respond to a crisis, effectively communicate up, and continually improve our strategy.

Problems are nothing but wake-up calls for creativity.

—**GERHARD GSCHWANDTNER**

CHAPTER 8

Troubleshooting

I N MY ROLE as a network operations director, I've encountered numerous challenges that have required me to troubleshoot solutions. Among the most common troubleshooting problem areas are (1) identifying the root cause of an issue, (2) managing time constraints effectively, (3) communicating with team members, and (4) ensuring long-term sustainability.

First, pinpointing the exact root cause of a problem can be challenging, especially in a complex network environment. It requires thorough analysis and often means sifting through layers of data to isolate the underlying issue.

Second, time constraints add pressure to the troubleshooting process. There's a delicate balance between resolving an issue swiftly and ensuring that the solution is comprehensive and sustainable in the long run. I've learned that if I rush through troubleshooting, it can lead to temporary fixes that may not address the underlying problems adequately.

Third, effective communication is also incredibly important during troubleshooting efforts. Coordinating with team members, stakeholders, and possibly external vendors requires clear and concise communication if you want to get everyone on the same page and working toward a common goal.

Fourth, somehow a leader needs to balance urgency with maintaining business continuity. While you have to address issues promptly, it's just as important not to disrupt ongoing operations unnecessarily. However, this requires careful prioritization and decision-making to minimize downtime and mitigate the impact of your troubleshooting efforts on business operations.

Navigating all of these challenges becomes even more complex because of the diverse skill sets and varying approaches within the team. After all, each team member may have a different perspective on how to solve the same problem, so it's up to leaders to coordinate their efforts toward a unified solution.

Ultimately, the goal of all troubleshooting is to prioritize the customer's needs and makes certain that business operations remain functional and sustainable. That requires delving into the root cause of the problem while, at the same time, considering the broader implications and long-term viability of the solution.

Common Troubleshooting Mistakes

When it comes to troubleshooting problems, I've identified seven common mistakes that leaders make:

- Focusing excessively on identifying the root cause rather than attempting to implement a resolution.
- Jumping to conclusions without fully investigating the problem, which can lead to wasted time and resources, as well as incorrect solutions.
- A lack of communication, which can hinder the troubleshooting process, as it prevents effective coordination among team members.
- Inadequate documentation, which makes it difficult to track progress and learn from past experiences, impeding future troubleshooting efforts.
- Failure to involve the right people, which means critical expertise may be overlooked, resulting in incomplete or ineffective solutions.
- Focusing solely on symptoms rather than addressing the underlying cause, which perpetuates recurring issues, prolonging downtime and customer dissatisfaction.
- Adding stress to the troubleshooting team by focusing only on the negative during discussions.

Each of these mistakes can hinder the resolution of technical issues and worsen the impact on customers and operations. Therefore, leaders need to remain vigilant and avoid falling into any of these traps. Let's look at each of them in some depth.

Obsessed with the Root Cause

Whenever I've been involved in troubleshooting issues, I've noticed that leaders tend to focus excessively on identifying the root cause rather than attempting to implement a resolution. This tendency becomes most apparent when a leader is faced with a straightforward issue, such as a router failure.

In these kinds of situations, leaders will often gather technical resources and furiously begin trying to diagnose the cause of the device's failure, rather than trying to resolve the issue swiftly to minimize customer impact. For example, let's suppose a core service like messaging stops functioning. Many leaders, in my experience, become fixated on uncovering the reason why the messaging service stopped instead of immediately implementing an alternate solution, such as rerouting traffic to another site.

I encountered this exact crisis when I worked in Burbank. However, when our messaging service went down, leaders moved swiftly to address the problem for customers by rerouting traffic. They didn't bother getting bogged down in determining the exact cause of the issue until a fix had been implemented.

If you focus on finding the root cause, it can overshadow the urgency of solving the problem. Customers don't care about the root cause. They just want your service to function. So prioritize finding a solution and then worry about finding the root cause and addressing it.

Jumping to Conclusions

While many leaders obsess over finding the root cause of a problem, other leaders assume they already know the root cause of a problem without conducting a thorough investigation. This tendency can result in a significant waste of time and resources, and it often leads to incorrect solutions being implemented.

Don't make any assumptions before you fully understand the issue. Otherwise, you can do more harm than good. I've witnessed firsthand the negative consequences of this approach, and it's never a favorable outcome. Resist the temptation to jump to conclusions and instead take the time to conduct a thorough investigation to ensure accurate problem-solving.

Lack of Communication

When leaders fail to communicate clearly and consistently with their team and stakeholders, they risk overlooking important information that could significantly expedite problem resolution. It's a lesson I've learned time and time again throughout my career: effective communication is truly indispensable in troubleshooting.

You may *think* you're communicating, but if your team and other stakeholders don't get the message, then you're not doing a good enough job. As George Bernard Shaw put it, "The single biggest problem in communication is the illusion that it has taken place."

Inadequate Documentation

Leaders who fail to document their troubleshooting efforts often struggle to replicate their successes or learn from their failures. Personally, I have come to appreciate the value of documenting troubleshooting immensely, as it provides an invaluable resource for future troubleshooting.

Now, that wasn't always the case. In my early years, I didn't always prioritize proper documentation. However, over time,

I realized its importance, especially in keeping team members aligned and preventing misunderstandings. As I transitioned into a leadership role, I recognized that clear documentation not only aids in learning and replicating success but also creates better communication and collaboration among team members.

Documenting each step of the troubleshooting process significantly reduces the likelihood that people will make assumptions or jump to conclusions. The docume ntation becomes a reliable reference point that enables you and your team to track progress, identify patterns, and make informed decisions based on solid evidence. In my time as a leader, it has become an indispensable tool in my approach to troubleshooting that contributes to individual growth and team cohesion.

Failing to Involve the Right People

Effective troubleshooting is truly a collaborative effort. No single person or group possesses all the ideas, answers, or solutions. Therefore, as a leader, particularly if you're a director or frontline manager, you have to make sure you involve the right people in the troubleshooting process. If you fail to engage the right people, vital information might be overlooked, and key solutions might get missed.

Reflecting on my own past experiences where troubleshooting didn't go well, I've often found that if I'd reached out to additional teams or experts, we could have potentially saved valuable time and minimized the impact of whatever issue we were dealing with.

Whether you seek input from specialized teams or involve stakeholders from different departments, just make sure you always assemble the most effective troubleshooting team possible. Each person brings unique insights and expertise to the table that will contribute to a more comprehensive and successful resolution of the problem. Collaboration is the central to effective troubleshooting, and involving the right people is essential to its success.

Focusing on Symptoms, Not the Cause

Focusing solely on symptoms rather than addressing the underlying cause is another common trap in troubleshooting. I've seen a tendency in many leaders to only tackle the surface-level issues without delving into the root cause because it seems quicker and easier, but they often find themselves caught in a cycle of recurring problems. You have to identify and resolve the root cause to prevent the issue from resurfacing.

This often happens with software bugs. It's easy to patch up what *seems* to be the problem, only to have it reappear later on. This can become a frustrating and counterproductive cycle if leaders fall into the habit of applying quick fixes without investing the necessary effort to truly understand and address the root cause of an issue.

Resist the temptation to focus solely on symptoms. Instead, invest the time and effort to uncover and remedy the underlying cause. By doing so, you can break free from the cycle of recurring problems and foster long-term stability and efficiency within your system.

Bringing Stress to the Troubleshooting Team

Recently, I had an experience where a leader came to a meeting with the troubleshooting team and added a whole bunch of stress to what had been an otherwise productive conversation. We were trying to figure out a network issue, and rather than staying calm and helping the team find the problem, he kept emphasizing the impact it was making on the network. He focused on the negative with a lot of doom-and-gloom talk and stressed out the team to such a degree that it hindered the discussion.

Leaders who do this are a bit like surgeons freaking out to their patients about the operation they're about to perform, or worse yet, constantly waking the patient up in the middle of an operation to complain that things aren't going according to plan.

"Oh, man, your spine is going to be so *messed up* after this procedure! This is horrible! You're going to be in so much agony! Do you *realize* how much this is going to hurt?"

Nobody wants a surgeon like that. The same goes for leaders. Nobody wants a leader who constantly emphasizes the negative. They *need* a leader who will keep everyone calm, cool, and collected so they can make progress and solve problems. In particular, network teams must remain calm if they're going to get the network healthy again, and it's on leaders to set the tone. You may be feeling stressed out or worried or near panic, but you can't dump this negativity on your team. As the old quote from Lao Tzu says, "Leadership is the ability to hide your panic from others."

Remain Vigilant and Open

Ultimately, leaders, especially operations directors like myself, need to remember that both answers and problems may still be undiscovered. When troubleshooting, complexity often presents itself in multiple layers that need to be thoroughly unraveled before a solution can be found. Rarely is this process a straightforward, one-size-fits-all scenario. Instead, issues tend to be multifaceted and deeply rooted, which demands open-mindedness, curiosity, and persistence in the search for the root cause.

Always remain vigilant and open to the possibility that there are still undiscovered factors that need to be identified. Embrace this mindset, and you will increase your chances of not only identifying solutions that address immediate problems but also implementing measures to prevent their recurrence in the future. This proactive approach will help you maintain operational stability and efficiency over the long term.

With that in mind, here are some tips I've found useful for identifying undiscovered problems and seeking answers, based on my own experience and industry. While this applies specifically to being a network operations directory, there are broader principles that apply to many different industries and leadership roles.

> Be careful believing you are better than you are. You will miss what someone smarter than you has to say.
>
> **—JESSE COOK,**
> Director of Network Operations

Continuously Monitor Network Performance

I always encourage leaders in my industry to maintain a continuous monitor of their network performance. Make sure your team is closely observing network performance metrics, keeping an eye out for any unusual behavior or deviations from the norm.

This proactive approach will help you catch any potential issues before they escalate into significant problems.

Over the past three years, I've seen some remarkable advancements in leveraging machine learning for this specific purpose. By harnessing machine learning capabilities, we're now able to monitor our networks with unprecedented granularity and detect deviations and anomalies that might otherwise go unnoticed. Our investment in this technology has proven invaluable as it allows us to identify and address issues before they have a chance to escalate. We're able to stay ahead of potential problems and maintain network stability more effectively than ever before.

Stay Up to Date

Staying up to date with industry trends and best practices will help you be more effective at both troubleshooting and decision-making. When you're well informed about the latest developments in your industry and understand current best practices, you can more readily anticipate potential issues before they arise and make informed decisions when troubleshooting. This helps you incorporate innovative approaches and forward-thinking strategies so you can stay ahead of potential challenges.

Leverage the collective experience and expertise of your teams to prevent issues from occurring. For instance, before implementing changes, I always conduct thorough failover testing with my team, seamlessly moving traffic between geo-redundant sites and performing tests to verify smooth operations.

By regularly assessing industry trends and adopting best practices, you gain insights into how other organizations manage similar challenges. This allows you to learn from their experiences and adapt strategies to protect your customers and maintain business continuity effectively. And by understanding and implementing these best practices, you maintain operational excellence, which helps you deliver a seamless experience to your customers.

Develop Deep Understanding

It's important to develop a deep understanding of your network infrastructure. Invest time in comprehending the intricacies of how your network infrastructure operates, inside and out. This includes familiarizing yourself with the terminology and ensuring you can navigate through the network architecture effectively.

In my own experience, while I may not be an engineer, I've accumulated extensive knowledge about how different components connect and interact with each other. This understanding allows me to provide guidance and coordinate with the appropriate support teams when issues arise.

Conduct Regular Audits

Conduct regular, thorough audits of your network infrastructure so you can more readily identify potential issues and, perhaps most importantly, vulnerabilities before they escalate into major problems. At my company, I oversee a dedicated team that is responsible for conducting these audits meticulously. We utilize various techniques, such as configuration compliance checks, to assure adherence to our standards and identify any deviations promptly.

Our continuous auditing processes, including checks for golden configurations and configuration compliance, enable us to maintain the integrity and security of our network. By identifying and addressing issues proactively, you can prevent potential disruptions and safeguard against security threats, ensuring the reliability and resilience of your network infrastructure.

Leverage Automation Tools

As a network operations director, I have witnessed (and utilized) the evolution of automation, machine learning, and AI. These technologies are intertwined, with automation feeding normalized data into machine learning models, and AI acting as an easy input to kick off task automation.

By using automation in leadership, I can complete repetitive processes that are normally done by team members, freeing up their time to focus on more strategic tasks. Machine learning is an amazing tool that helps me detect deviations in data by correlating multiple data sources simultaneously and notifies me when deviations occur.

Now, when it comes to using AI, I recommend ensuring that your company has a solid and secure structure around it. With AI, I am able to feed in multiple data sets and query the data to get a human response. Just imagine having your team's processes fed into an AI system tied to machine learning and looking at data sets. You can ask it questions, and it can pull all of that data together, making your team more efficient in their roles.

Incorporating automation tools into our processes has been a significant focus for me over the past five years or so, and I anticipate this trend will only continue to grow. Automation tools play a key role in identifying any potential issues and streamlining our troubleshooting processes, which allows our teams to concentrate on tackling more complex issues.

I can't emphasize this enough: the impact of automation, especially in troubleshooting, is remarkable. It simplifies tasks that would otherwise require considerable time and manpower. For instance, if a telco circuit experiences a failure, automation tools can swiftly detect the issue, gather pertinent information, generate a ticket, and notify the appropriate parties for a resolution. It tracks the progress of the ticket, conducts checks upon restoration, and makes certain that customer traffic is seamlessly restored—all without any manual intervention.

The efficiency and speed of automation are truly remarkable. These tools enable troubleshooting to occur in near real time, often resolving issues faster than humanly possible. It has been incredible to witness how automation enhances our troubleshooting capabilities so we can address problems swiftly and efficiently, ultimately ensuring a seamless experience for our customers.

Culture of Collaboration

In my opinion, the most important advice I can offer is to foster a culture of collaboration and knowledge sharing. Encouraging teams to openly share their knowledge and collaborate on troubleshooting not only accelerates the identification of potential issues but also cultivates a more efficient and cohesive team dynamic. From a business standpoint, this approach will lead to the development of a more resilient network.

When teams are empowered to share their insights and work together to find solutions, innovative ideas emerge. In my experience, teams usually end up proposing measures that prevent similar issues from occurring in the future, many of which come at minimal cost. Prioritizing collaboration and knowledge sharing among your teams are, as I said, the most impactful things you can do, and if you only follow one of the strategies I've recommended in this chapter, follow this one.

> The right team finds an easy fix for a complex problem.
>
> —JESSE COOK,
> Director of Network Operations

A Playbook for Initial Engagement

Personally, the most successful overall approach I've witnessed in troubleshooting is when leaders provide their teams with a predefined playbook for initial engagement. This playbook outlines specific actions they are to take in response to common issues. For instance, during a network outage, the playbook might tell them that the first immediate action is to redirect traffic away from the affected area.

This redirection can take various forms, such as routing traffic to geo-redundant sites, rerouting traffic between equipment, or implementing dynamic routing strategies to bypass potential problem areas. The key here is to prioritize maintaining service for the customer above all else.

By leveraging failover mechanisms before fully understanding the root cause of the issue, leaders demonstrate a commitment to providing uninterrupted service for customers. This approach effectively puts the customer's needs first, with the understanding that troubleshooting can occur afterward.

In my observation, this proactive approach to troubleshooting complex issues has consistently yielded positive results. It prioritizes customer satisfaction and operational continuity while simultaneously providing steps to identify and address underlying issues.

Today is your opportunity to build the tomorrow you want.

—KEN POIROT

CHAPTER 9

Building for Tomorrow, Not Today

L EADERS SHOULD FOCUS on building for tomorrow because the landscape of our world is in constant flux. Businesses must continually adapt and evolve to remain relevant and, perhaps more significantly, to stay competitive in the marketplace. By looking ahead and investing in emerging technologies, leaders—and especially directors like myself—can effectively position our organizations for future success and expansion.

If you fail to anticipate and prepare for future advancements, you risk falling behind competitors who are more agile and forward-thinking. Ultimately, prioritizing building for tomorrow helps to preserve the long-term sustainability and prosperity of your organization and lays the groundwork today to thrive in the ever-changing landscape of tomorrow. As President Lincoln said, "The most reliable way to predict the future is to create it."

There are a few distinct ways in which leaders sometimes falter in building for the future, so let's dive into them. From what I've observed, there are three primary ways leaders fail to build for tomorrow:

- Lack of Vision
- Resistance to Change
- Failure to Invest in Innovation

First, there's a common problem of leaders lacking a vision for the future. It's easy for leaders to get caught up in what they're doing now and become overly fixated on hitting short-term goals, overlooking the importance of planning for the future. But you need to have a clear vision of where you intend to steer your organization in the long run.

Personally, I believe in looking at least eighteen months ahead, preferably extending to three years, to chart a strategic course. Without a robust vision that reaches that far into the future, strategic decision-making becomes challenging.

Second, resistance to change is another common problem. Some leaders are averse to change, and they prefer the comfort of the status quo. However, this reluctance often leads to missed opportunities and an inability to adapt to evolving market dynamics. Organizations that resist change risk falling behind competitors who embrace innovation and forward-looking initiatives. As Jack Welch advised, "Change before you have to."

Third, there's also the danger of failing to invest in innovation. Merely discussing the importance of innovation isn't enough. Leaders must be proactive about allocating resources and capital to drive innovation initiatives. However, many fall short in this regard. They hesitate to invest in new technologies and processes that could propel the organization forward, and this lack of investment undermines their competitiveness and hinders their ability to keep pace with industry changes.

Of these three common issues, the failure to invest in innovation stands out as the most significant. It's relatively easy to articulate your future aspirations for innovation, but without tangible investments, these aspirations remain hollow. To truly build for tomorrow, you must align your strategic vision with concrete investments in innovation, whether in terms of human capital, financial resources, or technological infrastructure. It's not enough to talk the talk; you must walk the walk and commit to the strategic investments necessary for future success.

Left in the Dust

Reflecting on my own experiences, the one example of failing to build for tomorrow that readily comes to mind is the evolution of BlackBerry devices. I vividly recall a time when BlackBerry devices were considered revolutionary. They offered an innovative solution that captivated customers, myself included. With a BlackBerry, you could have everything you needed at your fingertips. The devices offered robust security, as well as user-friendly email integration and cutting-edge messaging capabilities.

In January 2010, at the height of its popularity, BlackBerry commanded 43 percent of the smartphone market.[4] However, despite their initial success and amazing early growth, the company eventually faltered. By January 2013, they only held onto 5.9 percent of the market. So what happened to cause such a precipitous decline?

Over time, BlackBerry shifted its focus toward an enterprise vision and lost sight of what its customers truly desired. They became complacent, convinced that they understood their customers' needs and preferences. Ultimately, this led to a stagnation in innovation and a failure to adapt to changing consumer demands. Meanwhile, competitors like Apple seized the opportunity to fulfill those evolving customer needs, leaving BlackBerry in the dust.

Today, BlackBerry devices are virtually nonexistent in the market. At the time of this writing, BlackBerry phones account for about 0.05 percent of the global smartphone market,[5] one of the starkest examples of the consequences of failing to innovate and invest in meeting customer expectations. If you want to avoid the same unfortunate trajectory, you have to remain agile and responsive to customer needs, and you must always be mindful of the perils of complacency in the face of evolving market dynamics.

Strategies for Resourcing Talent

Of course, if you're going to stay focused on building for the future, then you need to resource talent that can usher in new technologies into your operations. I recommend the following strategies.

First, I prioritize candidates who demonstrate a genuine passion for innovation and a strong desire for continuous learning. One avenue I've explored with success is recruiting from universities renowned for their robust technology programs. By bringing in fresh graduates, we inject our team with new perspectives and approaches to problem-solving. These individuals often possess the latest knowledge and insights, which can catalyze innovation within our organization.

Moreover, attending network events and industry conferences has proven fruitful for discovering candidates with the requisite skills and experiences. Engaging with professionals in these settings allows us to tap into talent pools that align closely with our technological needs.

During the interview process, I make it a point to seek out these qualities as they are essential for driving technological advancements within our team, and I make a concerted effort to delve into candidates' experiences with new and emerging technologies. I also inquire about their adaptability to change and their ability to thrive in collaborative work environments. These discussions offer valuable insights into a candidate's readiness to integrate new technologies into our operations.

Finally, I emphasize the importance of ongoing training and professional development opportunities for our existing staff. By investing in the continuous growth of our team members, we not only attract individuals who are eager to learn and evolve but also retain our top talent. This dual approach ensures that we are well-equipped to embrace new technologies while also nurturing the talents and skills of our current workforce.

> Building a high performing team takes consistency, agreed-upon common goals and values, with positive reinforcement along the journey.
> —BRIAN KING,
> CIO and COO of Technology

Incorporating New Technology

Incorporating new technology into existing staff can indeed pose significant challenges for leaders, regardless of your position within the organization. The natural human resistance to change is not limited to leaders. Your team members feel it too. But it's important to navigate through this resistance effectively to achieve your desired outcomes.

To safeguard a smooth transition, I recommend involving the staff in the decision-making process from the outset. By giving them a seat at the table, we empower them to voice their opinions and concerns, which contributes to a sense of ownership and buy-in toward the new technology. In this way, we make sure that everyone understands the necessity of the change and is aligned with its objectives.

Equally important is providing comprehensive training to the team to familiarize them with the new technology and its functionalities. There may be a bit of potential reluctance from some leaders because of costs, but investing in proper training is nonnegotiable. It equips team members with the necessary skills and knowledge to effectively utilize the new tools, which maximizes their potential and contributes to the desired outcome.

Finally, patience is key throughout this whole process. Remember: change takes time, so you should allow your teams the space to adapt to the new technology at their own pace. When you acknowledge the change curve and embrace a patient approach, you create a supportive environment where team members feel encouraged to explore and embrace the new technology without feeling rushed or overwhelmed.

This approach has been instrumental in my experience as a leader, and it has allowed me to successfully integrate new technology while keeping our teams motivated and engaged throughout the transition.

Reimagining Our Infrastructure

I've had many instances throughout my career where I had to incorporate new technology with existing staff. One that stands out is our transition to Voice over Long Term Evolution (VoLTE), a then-revolutionary high-speed wireless communication standard. It was a significant shift in our telecommunications infrastructure but one that ultimately proved to be more efficient for both our business and our consumers.

For over two decades of my career, we had operated with voice as its own technology type, with dedicated connections to cell phones. However, VoLTE revolutionized this approach by integrating voice calls into the data network, streamlining the process and improving the overall efficiency and call quality for our customers.

However, this transition required us to entirely reimagine our infrastructure. We moved away from traditional individual computers to a cloud-based architecture and consolidated all information into one centralized location with interconnected applications. This was a massive departure from the familiar systems our staff had been accustomed to for years.

To successfully navigate this change, I made sure our staff was involved in the decision-making process from the beginning. We engaged them in discussions about the technologies we were exploring and sought their input on how these changes would impact their roles and operations. This collaborative approach helped build buy-in and understanding from the outset.

Training played a critical role in this transition. We invested heavily in providing comprehensive training on the new architecture and cloud-based technologies, which included teaching our team members the fundamentals of cloud computing and data pathways, as well as how VoLTE functions within the new framework. It was a lengthy process that spanned years, but ultimately it was a necessary change that made sure our staff was equipped and ready to embrace the change.

The most challenging aspect of the transition was exercising patience throughout the entire process. As leaders, we allowed our teams to have the time and space they needed to adjust to the new technology at their own pace. For many of our team members, they were being asked to let go of decades-old practices and embrace entirely new ways of working. Some people adapted quickly, while others required more time, but in the end, every engineer found their footing and embraced the new technology.

By following these steps—(1) engaging staff in decision-making, (2) providing comprehensive training, and (3) exercising patience—we successfully incorporated the new technology while keeping our team motivated and engaged throughout the transition. Today, VoLTE is a standard technology used by providers worldwide, and our organization's successful adoption of it stands as a testament to our strategic planning and readiness for change.

Keeping One Eye Forward

You need to keep one eye forward, looking to the future at all times. Here are some tips for doing so:

First, keep yourself well informed. This means staying updated on the latest trends in technology by attending technical conferences, networking with industry professionals, and engaging with vendors to learn about emerging technologies.

Network with peers in your field who can offer valuable insights into the challenges they're facing and how they're addressing them, which will, in turn, help you identify opportunities for innovation within your own organization.

Second, be open to change. Embracing new technologies and processes requires a willingness to adapt and experiment. As a director, you need to remain open-minded and receptive to new ideas, even if they disrupt the status quo. Encourage your team to embrace change and be willing to explore new tools and approaches to problem-solving.

Finally, as we've touched on many times throughout this book, it's important to foster a culture of innovation within your organization. To successfully implement new technologies, you need a team that's willing to think creatively, take risks, and embrace new ideas. Encourage a culture of innovation by providing opportunities for training and professional development, keeping your team updated on the latest technologies, and leading by example.

When you demonstrate your own willingness to take risks and embrace change, you will inspire your team to do the same, creating an environment where innovation thrives.

- Stay updated on the latest trends in technology, especially in your industry.
- Be open to change and willing to adapt.
- Foster a culture of innovation within your organization.

Don't let the future pass you by. It's easy to get caught up in the day-to-day responsibilities of leading your team and lose sight of coming changes in your industry, so keep an eye on the road ahead. If you do, you will be ready to adapt and meet those changes with confidence.

Leadership is unlocking people's potential to become better.

—BILL BRADLEY

Leadership Is a Continual Investment

OVER THE COURSE of this book, I have tried to convey a few important messages to junior executives specifically, as well as to leaders at all levels. First and foremost, I have emphasized the importance of nurturing a positive company culture. I truly believe that this, above anything else you can do, will have the most significant impact on boosting motivation, productivity, and employee retention. Alongside a positive culture, I stressed the value of fostering collaboration and communication across teams and departments, as they are absolutely essential for building strong and effective teams.

Another theme we discussed is the art of delegation and prioritization. As a leader, you need to learn how to delegate tasks effectively so you can focus on the bigger picture and strategic planning. We also covered some strategies for getting your people not to meet goals but to surpass them by creating an environment of trust and providing opportunities for continuous learning.

Then we examined the importance of building and maintaining a strong technical talent pool so you can always address problems swiftly. And we looked at why it's so important to strike a delicate balance between innovation and stability.

Of course, no leadership book would be complete without a bit of advice on handling crises. When things don't go as planned, people depend on their leaders to stand up, take charge, and know how to pull people together to troubleshoot problems effectively. It's your job to stay calm, cool, and collected, not add to the stress by panicking or focusing solely on the negative.

As an operations director myself, I fully understand that things aren't always going to go right, and that's why it's so important to focus on troubleshooting. To that end, I shared some valuable insights on how to maintain focus under pressure and adopt a proactive approach to problem-solving. Remember: the right solution may yet be undiscovered, so make sure people feel safe to share ideas.

Finally, we ended our time by emphasizing the importance of looking ahead and building for tomorrow rather than solely focusing on the present. In our ever-evolving business landscape, leaders need to maintain a long-term vision. They must be willing to make the necessary investments, allocate the right resources, and develop appropriate strategies to meet the future if they're going to remain competitive.

Leadership Keys: An Overview

- Nurture a positive company culture.
- Foster collaboration and communication.
- Prioritize and delegate tasks.
- Inspire your team to surpass goals.
- Maintain a strong talent pool.
- Strike the right balance between innovation and stability.
- Have a plan for dealing with crises.
- Adopt a proactive approach to troubleshooting.
- Keep one eye focused on the future.

Feeling Overwhelmed?

Since I understand the struggles we all face as junior executive leaders, I realize some of you might be feeling overwhelmed and exhausted on the job these days. There's probably a lot on your plate, and there may be times when you wonder how long you can keep this up.

I'd like to share some final words of encouragement. Look, you're not alone in feeling this way. All leaders experience periods of burnout and may feel completely overwhelmed at times. This often happens during times of significant change, such as when a key employee leaves or when implementing new technologies that aren't wholly embraced by the team. Somehow, you have to find a balance between your work and personal life.

I know this can be challenging, especially when you're faced with a heavy workload, but I encourage you to find ways to carve out some time for yourself. Make regular time to pause, reflect, and recover.

At the same time, one of the biggest causes of frustration for junior executives is when you find yourself carrying messages from senior leaders down to your team that you don't necessarily agree with. No one likes to be the bearer of bad news, and junior executives often find themselves caught in the middle.

What can you do in that situation? I encourage you to take ownership of your message to the team while also understanding that your senior leaders own their message to the team as well. What do I mean by that? Well, the content of the message might be out of your hands. However, you can decide *how* you communicate it to your team. Maybe you need to soften the impact of a negative message by framing it with encouragement and a bit of hopefulness.

Do everything you can to foster a culture of trust within your team so you can rely on each other. Remember: you don't have to tackle everything alone. Your team can contribute valuable ideas and support, and when they're actively contributing, it's going to take a lot of the burden off your shoulders.

Learning to Lead

But maybe collaboration isn't your problem. Maybe overwork isn't your problem, or passing along messages from senior executives, or any of the other things I've mentioned. Instead, maybe your biggest problem is that you feel like you're not excelling in your role. You just don't feel like a very good or effective leader. If that's the case, I recommend the following three steps:

First, as with any problem, try to identify the root cause. Why do you feel this way? What is making you ineffective as a leader? Try to understand what is holding you back, whether it's a lack of motivation, direction, or struggles with specific tasks or projects. Once you've pinpointed the cause, you know where to focus and start working toward a solution.

Second, seek feedback and guidance from trusted mentors and colleagues. Sometimes, when we're feeling stuck, hindered, or ineffective, it's hard to see the bigger picture, but seeking input from others can provide valuable insights that will help you navigate your situation with clarity. Reach out to people you trust and ask for their perspectives and suggestions on how to move forward and become a better leader.

Finally, focus on continuous learning and development. A good leader provides opportunities for growth and learning for their team, but they also create those opportunities for themselves. As a junior executive, especially if you're a network operations director, if you want to stay relevant and engaged in your role, it's going to require ongoing skill enhancement. Attend conferences, workshops, or take online courses to broaden your knowledge and improve your skills. Additionally, seek out opportunities to work on new and challenging projects to keep yourself motivated and engaged.

By following these steps, I'm confident you can overcome feelings of being stuck or ineffective in your role, even as you focus on addressing the root causes. Always remember: it's OK to seek support and continuously invest in your own professional growth. You matter too. A leader can't properly take care of their team if they're not also taking care of themselves.

You can do this! Now, get out there and lead!

ACKNOWLEDGMENTS

I would like to acknowledge the following people for the inspiration, motivation, and impact on me, my career, and my life:

First of all, my wife, Karen Cook; my daughter, Karly Phipps; and my son, Conner Cook, who all inspired me to take this journey.

Over the years, I've had the pleasure of working for and with many leaders who helped guide me. Below are a few callouts I would like to acknowledge.

Angel Marchand, senior director of Network Operations, for giving me the opportunity to enter the world of telecommunications. I will always be grateful for his unwavering support and guidance, which helped me take the first step toward leadership.

Brian King, chief information officer and chief operations officer of Technology, for his dedication to ensuring that our teams always prioritize customer satisfaction. His passion for his work has created a culture of collaboration, trust, and success within his team. I am thankful for his accountability toward my needs and for setting an excellent example for all of us.

Joe Meyer, vice president of Network Operations, for his invaluable mentorship and guidance since the day we met. Joe's expertise and advice have been instrumental in helping me understand the fundamental principles of a director's role. I am genuinely grateful for his unwavering support and guidance, which have helped me become a better leader.

Amy Kellogg, vice president of Network Operations, for her exceptional mentorship and guidance during the brief period I had the privilege of working with her. Her leadership style was focused on empowering those around her to succeed, and her light continues to inspire me and those who had the opportunity to work with her.

Delroy Murray, vice president of Network Operations, for his leadership and mentorship. Delroy has challenged me to think differently and develop innovative solutions to problems. I have gained a wealth of leadership knowledge from him in a short time, and I am thankful for his guidance.

Keith Mathies, vice president of Network Operations, has been a shining light at every gathering. He is never afraid to speak his mind, and through our conversations, I have come to realize that employees are the backbone of a successful organization. Keith has taught me how to improve team culture, balance leadership expectations, and have fun along the way.

Stephanie Feiss, senior director of Network Operations, for her invaluable mentoring. Stephanie has challenged me to look beyond the technical aspects of problems and focus on the leadership perspective. Her guidance has expanded my view of team structures and approach to solving complex problems. I am truly grateful for her mentorship.

I would like to express my heartfelt gratitude to Jason Batchelder, director of Network Operations. Working under and with his leadership has been an absolute pleasure and a truly enriching experience. His mentorship has taught me the importance of balance in leadership. I have learned to consider the significance of every request before sending it out and to be mindful of my team's time. Thank you, Jason, for being an exceptional leader and for sharing your wisdom with me.

Finally, thank you to the publishing team—Jeff Miller, Will Severns, Trevor Waite, Donnel McLohon, and all the other individuals at Streamline who played an essential role in bringing this book to life. Your dedication, hard work, and support have been instrumental in making this project successful.

ABOUT THE AUTHOR

Jesse Cook is an experienced leader who has helped teams navigate the intricacies of the telecommunications industry over the course of his twenty-four-year career. Starting in the data center as an engineer, Jesse soon discovered his passion for leading and mentoring others—he finds nothing more fulfilling than seeing people take on challenges and excel. With two degrees under his belt, Jesse takes pride in honing his leadership skills as the technical world continues to evolve, and his goal is to help organizations evolve with it.

Want to learn more about leadership? Have a few more questions on the tactics and strategies discussed in this book? Head over to JesseLCook.com or reach out to the author directly at 321beach@gmail.com.

ENDNOTES

1 Nikki Morin and Heather Barrett, "Don't Confuse 'Being in the Office' With 'Culture,'" Gallup, September 28, 2022, https://www.gallup.com/workplace/401576/dont-confuse-office-culture.aspx.

2 Rob Stevens, "Proactive Delegation: A 7-Step Guide for Leaders," LinkedIn, September 22, 2023, https://www.linkedin.com/pulse/proactive-delegation-7-step-guide-leaders-rob-stevens/.

3 Abbey Lewis, "Good Leadership? It All Starts with Trust," Harvard Business Publishing, October 26, 2022, https://www.harvardbusiness.org/good-leadership-it-all-starts-with-trust/.

4 Ron Miller, "BlackBerry Phones Once Ruled the World, then the World Changed," TechCrunch, https://techcrunch.com/2022/01/03/blackberry-phones-once-ruled-the-world-then-the-world-changed/.

5 Siyam Adit, "The Importance of Evolving Product Design: A Case Study of BlackBerry's Rise and Fall," Medium, April 27, 2023, https://bootcamp.uxdesign.cc/the-importance-of-evolving-product-design-a-case-study-of-blackberrys-rise-and-fall-5c21ceaf395a.